CUBS WITH A DIFFERENCE

Stephen Andrews

Illustrated by Val Biro

Beaver Books

A Beaver Book
Published by Arrow Books Limited
17–21 Conway Street, London W1P 6JD
An imprint of the Hutchinson Publishing Group
London Melbourne Sydney Auckland Johannesburg
and agencies throughout the world

First published in 1972 by Hodder and Stoughton Children's Books
Beaver edition 1984
© Copyright text Piper's Ash Limited 1972
© Copyright illustrations Hodder and Stoughton Limited 1972

Set in Baskerville
Made and printed in Great Britain by
Anchor Brendon Limited, Tiptree, Essex

ISBN 09 933220 5

Contents

1

The 2nd Billington Pack

Akela stood still in the middle of the Pack, with his arms outstretched like a statue. He was a tall, healthy young man and, to judge by the Wood Badge he wore, a very experienced Scouter. He waited until every Cub was still and quiet, and then smartly he lowered his arms. At this signal, the Pack of Cubs squatted on their haunches. Some of the Cubs, like Christopher Clark, the newest Cub in the Pack, sat on the hall floor. Christopher, so called because he was born on Christmas day, was a cheerful little fellow, although he couldn't bear the sound of his name. He much preferred his nickname 'Nobby'.

'Akela! We'll do our best,' shrieked the Pack.

Then all the Cubs jumped up, not a bit in time; in fact they moved like a string of yo-yos. The Duty Sixer stood to attention and waited for his fellow Cubs to stand still, or rather to stand reasonably still, for some Cubs, like Nobby Clark, scratched their legs, twisted their faces and swayed like poplar trees in a high wind.

Georgie White, the other new Cub, who incidentally had been born on St George's day, stood to attention. Like Akela, he was rock steady, with his head held erect and his little chin jutting out. Georgie had hair like strands of gold and blue eyes which sparkled like pale sapphires. His nickname was 'Snowy', partly because of his fair complexion, and partly because of his surname.

'Cubs! Do your best!' ordered the Duty Sixer.

The Cubs saluted, Snowy like a guardsman on his first parade duty. Nobby scratched his head, and wondered what all this ceremony was about.

'We will do our best,' replied the Cubs.

Snowy spoke from his heart. Nobby squawked like a parrot, then after the Union Flag had been slowly lowered, the Cubs broke the circle to go to the cloakroom for their coats.

'See you next Friday, lads,' called Akela. 'Don't forget to bring your sausages for a fry-up.'

'Good night, everybody!'

Snowy and Nobby left the headquarters together. They were the greatest of pals, with ties of friendship stronger than family ties.

'How do you like the Cubs, Nobby?' asked Snowy. 'Did you think it would be like this, with all the games, and all those useful things like tying knots, and all the Cubs' jokes and all that?'

'I think it's fine, but I ripped the seat of my

trousers when I squatted for the grand Howl.
Look at the rip! You can see my underpants!'

'Nobody will notice the rip in your trousers if
you walk with your hands behind your back.
The Duke of Edinburgh often walks with his
hands behind his back.'

'Good idea!' said Nobby, walking on with
his hands behind his back. 'If he had a hole in
his pants, nobody would ever know, would
they? Akela's a good sport, isn't he?' went on
Nobby. ' He knows everything about Scouting.
I bet he was a good Cub Scout when he was a
boy.'

'I suppose so,' said Snowy, thoughtfully, as he
walked on. 'I think it must be very difficult to be
a good Cub, you know, Nobby, a really good
Cub, I mean, although I'm not really clear
myself what a good Cub is.'

'Dad says if I want to be good, all I have to do
is the opposite to what I normally do.'

'Is that why you have your cap on back to

front? I don't know whether you're coming or going.'

'I haven't, have I?' Nobby straightened his cap. 'It was only on sideways.'

Nobby pushed the fringe of his thick ginger hair out of his pale green eyes, and in doing so, unconsciously knocked his cap sideways again, before he put his hands behind his back to cover the rip in his trousers.

'Why, no boy can be really perfect,' said Nobby. 'I bet my dad wasn't perfect when he was my age, although he pretends he was. You know, Snowy, he's always telling me my school reports are terrible, but he has never shown me one of his reports. Mum says I must take after my dad, for if his reports were as good as he says they were, he would have kept them to show us. I bet he tore them up the morning he got them, if possible before Grandad saw them.'

Snowy laughed, but seriously he wanted to be a good Cub, as good a Cub as Nelson was a sailor, and *he* loved the Navy, England and God, in that order, and he was prepared to die for them; or as Florence Nightingale was a nurse, and *she* gave up marriage to look after the poor, sick people in the hospital slums.

They walked on in silence. Suddenly Nobby snapped his fingers and stopped Snowy. He pointed at a policeman standing near the pedestrian crossing.

'Let's tell that policeman the time,' said Nobby earnestly.

'The time? Why? Why should we tell him the time? What are you talking about?'

'You've heard that old song, haven't you? "If you want to know the time, ask a policeman." '

'Well?' Snowy was confused.

'Well, if you tell him the time, he'll know the time for when someone asks him. That would be a good deed.'

'He'll give you time if you're not careful – in prison.'

The Cubs crossed over the pedestrian crossing.

'Caught any good crooks lately?' Nobby yelled at the policeman.

'What did you say?' said the policeman, coming up behind Nobby.

'I said, "Read any good books lately?",' said Nobby, scampering away.

'Good night, officer,' said Snowy, trying to keep the peace.

''Night, boys.'

The policeman turned away. Snowy caught up with Nobby who was hiding behind a hedge.

'Why did you say that? You'll get us locked up.'

Nobby walked on with his hands in his pockets. 'He wouldn't lock me up, Snowy. I'm his friend. Dad says the best way to make friends is to make people laugh. Didn't you see that policeman smile? He nearly swallowed his chin-strap. He smiled and pretended he didn't want to smile, which is the last thing he should have done if he wanted to hide his smile.'

'Ah, come on,' said Snowy.

The Cubs walked on, with Snowy still deep in thought. Nobby was a born comedian, and Snowy enjoyed his friendship. It would be difficult to take Cub Scouting seriously with Nobby around, that's for sure, for every time he opened his mouth, he put his foot in it. Not that Snowy would ever think of ditching his friend. That was the last thing he would do.

Suddenly Nobby turned back and scratched at something beneath the privet hedge, as if he were digging for a bone.

'Puss, puss, puss, puss, puss,' said Nobby,

snapping his fingers and trying to crawl under the hedge.

Snowy bent down and saw a little wire-haired terrier, which was more wire-hair than terrier. Its hair hung down in long strands over its eyes and covered all its face. The little animal was no more than a few weeks old, wet through, and shivering violently.

'That's a pup, not a puss,' said Snowy. He stroked the little animal, which licked his hand. 'Poor thing, it must be starving, and it's drenched. What's it doing out at this time of night? Dogs shouldn't be allowed out by themselves.'

'It may be lost,' suggested Nobby. 'Cats shouldn't be allowed out by themselves unless they're on a lead.'

'Dogs, you mean.'

'Cats! Dogs, I mean.'

Snowy looked at the collar. 'It's got a name-tag with an inscription on it. It's . . . it's called Poggles.'

'Puddles? That's a funny name for a dog, even if it is wet.'

'Poggles!' said Snowy. 'Poggles Williamson, it says here.'

'Oh! Poggles the poodle. That's a good name. Hey, Snowy, let's take it to the policeman on duty. He'll look after it if it's lost. The police don't only chase crooks, you know. They like to help people when they can. Maybe they'll train it to be a tracker dog. Maybe they'll train it to catch crooks.'

Snowy could not imagine that little thing ever chasing anything bigger than a ball of wool, but he did not want to encourage Nobby to start an argument.

'It's not lost if we've found it, is it?' Snowy looked on the other side of the name-tag. 'It lives in Parkfield Road, that's just around the corner. Come on, the police have plenty of work to do without us giving them more. We'll take Poggles home. Let me borrow your neckerchief for Poggles, will you, Nobby?' Snowy whipped off his own neckerchief.

Nobby took off his neckerchief and draped it round Poggles's neck.

'Poggles looks stupid wearing a big neckerchief.'

'It's not for it to wear, it's to make a dog-lead.'

Snowy tied the two neckerchiefs together and looped them round the little dog's collar. It may not seem to be important to find a lost dog, but no doubt it was very important to the dog, and if Snowy could take it home, it would relieve its suffering.

'Come on, Poggles, we'll see you home.'

The Cubs ran the little dog down Parkfield Road, and they found the right house. Mrs Williamson was the little old lady who lived in the big house all alone. She wasn't very popular with her neighbours, for she was always complaining about how people these days make a nuisance of themselves. It was hard to blame her entirely, for she had had her front window broken twice by boys playing football in the street, and the cars and motor bikes which raced past her house made it dangerous for her to cross the street. Snowy walked up the drive, stretched up and rang the door-bell. Nobby stayed outside the gate and hid behind the privet hedge.

'Why . . . why are you staying out there?' asked Snowy, looking around and seeing Nobby's cap sticking above the hedge.

Nobby raised his head. 'She might think I kidnapped her precious little animal. I don't want to get the blame. I'm not a dog-stealer.'

The old lady answered the door. Immediately she saw her dog, her eyes lit up.

'Poggles, Poggles, my little Poggles. Where have you been? I've been looking for you all day. You have't had your din-dins yet.'

'Din-dins?' echoed a voice from behind the hedge.

'We found him down beside the main road hiding under a hedge,' said Snowy. 'He was shivering. I think he needs warming up.'

'Put him in the oven for half an hour then you'll have a little hot dog,' said a mysterious voice.

Snowy looked around but could see no one.

'What did you say, boy?' asked the old lady, picking up her dog and stroking him gently. 'There, there, there.'

'I didn't say anything.'

'I don't know what I would have done had you not found him. He must have come after me

when I went to the shops, lost me in the crowds and, poor thing, he couldn't find his way home. Couldn't you find your way home, my little Poggles? I heard the thunder rumbling in the distance, and I was afraid you might be left out all night in the pouring rain. Wait a minute, boy, let me get you something for your trouble. I think I have some apples left.'

The old lady went inside the house. As soon as she disappeared, or rather at the sound of the word 'apples', Nobby leapt out from behind the hedge, like a brigand from a forest ambush. He was waiting on the doorstep when the old lady reappeared. She looked at him in surprise.

'Who are you?' she asked.

'I'm Nobby. I found your scruffy little mongrel, I mean your nice little pup. He was lost and I found him, with Snowy's help.'

16

The old woman looked anxiously down the street.

'There aren't any more of you, are there?'

'No, no,' grinned Nobby, holding out his hand for an apple. 'Just the two of us.'

The old lady gave the boys an apple each, then went inside her house to feed her little dog. Snowy closed the garden gate.

'What's worse than finding a worm in your apple,' said Nobby, taking a bite out of his apple.

'I don't know,' said Snowy.

'Finding half a worm in your apple,' said Nobby, munching away like a donkey chewing a carrot.

'I wonder what other adventures we'll have in the Cubs, Nobby,' said Snowy. 'Plenty, I'm sure. There're lots of things we can do in the Cubs, Nobby, like camping, and collecting things, and photography and swimming.'

'Yeah!' said Nobby, spitting out a pip. 'If we do a good turn every day, we might end up like the older Cubs with lots of patches on our sleeves.'

'Patches, patches? What are you talking about?' Nobby looked at Snowy as if he were stupid.

'If you had your eyes open when the colour was lowered,' he said, 'you might have noticed the Duty Sixer who lowered the flag had a sleeve like my bike inner-tube, all patched up.'

'Patched up? What do you mean, patched up? He looked all right to me.'

'Didn't you notice? His sleeves were covered with little patches. An army of moths must have been at his old jersey.'

'Patches? Patches? They're not patches, they're badges.'

'Are they? All over his sleeves? So that's why they were all different colours, eh? I thought maybe his mum couldn't afford to darn his old jersey.'

Snowy threw up his hands. Nobby walked on, forgetting to hold his hands behind his back, so his shirt tail stuck out.

'Snowy, I'd give anything in the world to have one of those patches.'

'Talking of patches, Nobby, the first patch you'll need is one on your trousers.'

2

Fireman's lift

If the boys were hoping to find plenty to do in the Cubs, they were not to be disappointed. Their neighbours, the Scouts, were planning to raise money to buy a van to tour the continent in the summer, and although the Cubs had planned nothing more ambitious than a week-end camp in the Pennines, Akela had offered to help the Scouts raise the money they wanted, so that he could borrow the Scout van for his Cubs when the Scouts weren't using it. So every Saturday morning, some of the Cubs volunteered to go down to their headquarters to clean cars to raise the money required. The word soon spread round the village that the Cubs and Scouts were willing to do all sorts of odd jobs, and offers came in from all quarters. Mrs Hilton, a neighbour of the Clarks, asked Snowy and Nobby to come and see her if they wanted to earn twenty pence apiece.

Snowy stopped outside Mrs Hilton's house. Nobby trembled in terror.

'I've . . . I've changed my mind,' said Nobby, his eyes rolling like marbles.

'Changed your mind?' echoed Snowy. 'Don't you want to raise money for the Scout van?'

'But . . . but she has a baby.'

'Well.'

'She might ask me to take the baby for a walk. Oh, Snowy, if any of the Cubs saw me pushing a pram, they would never let me live it down. I'd . . . I'd be the biggest laugh since Coco the Clown.'

'What sort of job do you want to do?'

'Lots of things, such as sorting through comics to see if any pages are missing, or tasting lemonade to make sure it's not poisoned.'

Snowy laughed. 'That's what I call wishful thinking.'

'It's not wishbone thinking at all. You've heard of wine-tasters, haven't you? Well, there must be lemonade-tasters somewhere. That's just the job I'd like. I'd sit at the end of the conveyor belt and take a sip out of each bottle that goes by, to make sure no one's forgotten to put in the fizz. That's a very important job. I'd do that job for nothing. . . .'

Snowy walked through Mrs Hilton's car-port and pressed the back-door bell.

'I'll never be seen dead pushing a pram,' emphasised Nobby, sneaking in quietly and hiding behind the drain-pipe.

Mrs Hilton answered the door. She was obviously in the middle of her house-work. Her hair was in curlers. She wiped her hands on her apron.

20

'You said you wanted to see us, Mrs Hilton,' said Snowy, 'to do a job for you.'

'You can't do my ironing, can you? I've got a pile of ironing which will take me a month to get through.'

Nobby let out a yell, as if he was being strangled. Mrs Hilton poked her head out of the door.

'What's up with your friend? Is he having a fit?'

'No, Mrs Hilton. I think he just wants you to know he's hiding behind the drain-pipe.'

'Oh no, I don't!' growled Nobby.

'Well, since you can't do the ironing, you can polish the shoes. I'll get them out of the cupboard for you.'

Only then did Nobby show his face. He heaved a sigh of relief and came out of his hiding place. Mrs Hilton dumped a pile of shoes in the car-port and gave the shoe-polish bag to Snowy.

'Cor, you've got a lot of shoes, haven't you, missus?' goggled Nobby. 'You haven't got a giant centipede in the house, have you? I wouldn't like to darn all your socks.'

Mrs Hilton ignored him. 'There you are, boys. You've got everything you need. Make a good job of them and I'll give you twenty pence each to help you buy that van. Oh, I must get back to my ironing. I've left the iron on.' The baby cried upstairs. 'And now the baby's awake. Work is never done. Who would be a housewife?'

'Not me,' said Nobby quickly. 'That's for sure.'

'Ah, well!' Mrs Hilton shrugged her shoulders, went inside her house and closed the door.

'Whew!' said Nobby. 'For a moment I thought she might give us a sissy job. If she had asked us to take her baby for a walk, I would have been off like a shot.'

'Cleaning shoes isn't a sissy's job. Get stuck in, Nobby. I'll do the black, you can do the brown.'

Snowy brushed the dirt off his pile of black shoes. Nobby put some tan polish on his brush, rolled down his dirty, fawn sock and put some polish on his leg.

'What . . . what are you doing now?' groaned Snowy.

'I've got a hole in my sock,' explained Nobby. He pulled up his stocking so that the stained blotch on his leg lined up with the little hole in his sock. 'You can't see it now, not much, anyway.'

Nobby put some more polish on his brush and tackled the pile of brown shoes. He worked as if he had six hands, but by the time he had finished he had more polish on his hands than on his shoes. The polish was a rich, reddish brown, but on his skin it left a bright red stain. Nobby worked hard though, and after he had wiped the perspiration off his face with the polishing rag, he had the complexion of a North American Indian at the end of a hot summer in the dry hills of Dakota.

'Hot work, isn't it, Snowy?'

'You look like an Indian brave,' said Snowy.

'Do I?' said Nobby, rather flattered. He rubbed a shoe with the polishing rag. 'The Cherokees are after me . . .' he sang. 'They look mad . . .' Suddenly he stopped singing. He sniffed. 'What's that woman cooking?' he asked, nodding towards the back door. 'Roast sawdust?' He shrugged his shoulders. 'But I'm singing a happy song . . .'

Snowy finished polishing the black shoes, but his mind was not entirely on his job. He, too, was curious about the peculiar smell from the kitchen.

When they had finished, Nobby knocked on the back door – three short knocks, three long knocks and three short knocks. There was no immediate reply, so whilst they were waiting, Nobby trotted around the car-port, pretending he was riding a covered wagon.

'I'm practising for my acting test,' he

explained. 'Three wheels on my wagon, but I keep rolling along. . . .'

Suddenly Nobby stopped and looked at his reflection in the old mirror above the workbench.

'Yeowh!' he yelled when he saw his red-stained face. 'You're right, Snowy. I do look like a Red Indian.' He plucked up his courage and had another peep in the mirror. 'How!' he greeted his reflection. 'Big Sitting Bull is brave warrior, fears no one but Running Water. How now brown cow!'

Snowy paid no attention to Nobby, for he was now quite alarmed about the smell of burning from inside the house. He banged on the door. Still there was no reply.

'I . . . I think we should go in,' he said.

He reached up and opened the door. Immediately a cloud of grey smoke billowed out through the doorway and enveloped him. Snowy stepped back as the acrid smell puffed out into the car-port and stung his nostrils.

'Fire, fire!' he coughed. 'Nobby, run, run . . . Telephone the police and fire-brigade.'

'Right-oh, down the slippery pole.'

Nobby shot off like a streak of lightning, Snowy soaked his neckerchief under the outside tap, tied it around his face, took a deep breath of fresh air, and groped his way into the smoke-filled house. This is how a hero in a boys' comic he had read had reacted.

Inside the lounge he saw Mrs Hilton lying on

the floor. In the corner of the room, the television set belched out a plume of smoke. Snowy unplugged the double sockets from the mains to disconnect the electric iron, fire and television set, then he pushed open the window to let out the smoke. Just then he saw Nobby running back.

'Nobby!' he shouted through the window.

'Hi, Snowy,' said Nobby. 'What number shall I dial for the police and fire-brigade?'

'999, don't you know?'

'Oh, I thought that was for an ambulance.' Nobby turned to go back.

'It's the same number for ambulance, police and fire-brigade, but never mind about that now, Nobby. Come in here and give me a hand.'

Nobby raised his neckerchief over his face and climbed in through the window.

'The masked bandits strike again!' he coughed. 'Cor, what's this place? Smoky Joe's?'

'Give me a hand to drag out Mrs Hilton. She's been overcome by the smoke.'

The Cubs took Mrs Hilton's arms and carefully pulled her out of the smoke-filled room, through the car-port and into the back garden. Snowy lowered his neckerchief.

'Ring for the fire-brigade now,' said Snowy. '999, remember.'

Nobby coughed violently. He rubbed the smoke out of his streaming eyes. '999, okay, Snowy,' he croaked, then without a thought for his own distress, he staggered off to get help.

The fresh air brought Mrs Hilton round. Snowy wiped her pale face with his wet neckerchief. She groaned, coughed and blinked open her eyes.

'Take it easy now, Mrs Hilton. The fire-brigade is on its way.'

'My baby! moaned Mrs Hilton. 'My baby . . . she's upstairs.'

'I'll get her!' said Snowy. 'You stay here. If you go inside, you'll be overcome by the fumes again, and without my friend I won't be able to help you.'

There wasn't much chance of Mrs Hilton going into the house again, even after her baby. Her lungs were still full of smoke. She was dizzy. She was incapable of standing on her feet. It was even an effort for her to cough.

Snowy pulled the neckerchief over his face and again went into the house. The smoke was as thick as ever, and Snowy took the precaution of closing the lounge door to stop the smoke spreading. Then, trying desperately not to rush or panic, he went upstairs to find the baby.

Finding the baby was no problem, for he was led to her by her cries. He found her sitting up in her cot. Snowy picked her up, draped a fine sheet over her head to protect her from the smoke, and carried her downstairs. Mrs Hilton had managed to pull herself to her feet. She clutched her child and took the sheet off her head. She was exhausted by her effort and staggered to the garden seat.

'My little darling,' she said. 'Oh dear, you're safe. I wouldn't have known what to do had I lost you. Our house is burning down, but that doesn't matter as long as you're safe.'

'Don't worry about the fire, Mrs Hilton,' said Snowy. 'I've unplugged the television set, so the fire will go out. It's . . . it's just smoking a bit now, that's all.'

'Yes, yes. Don't worry, my little one.' Mrs Hilton patted her baby's back. 'The nasty smoke won't get you any more.'

Almost immediately, Mrs Clark and Nobby came running up.

'Edna!' said Mrs Clark. 'Are you all right? Oh dear, you have had a nasty shock, haven't you? I'd die if anything like this happened to me. Are you sure you're all right?'

'Yes, yes, I think so, but the house is on fire.'

'The fire's gone out now,' said Snowy, after peering through the open window. 'It was the television set. It's just smouldering a little bit now.'

'You look dreadful, Edna,' said Mrs Clark. 'The fire-brigade is on its way. You can't do anything here, so come to my house and have a cup of tea.'

Mrs Hilton hugged her baby. She was helped to her feet by Mrs Clark and together they went off. Snowy and Nobby went to the front of the house to wait for the fire-brigade. When the fire-engines arrived, the fire chief jumped

out, drew out his axe and marched down the path.

'I didn't do it, honest!' said Nobby, jumping aside.

'If you did I'd chop off your head,' said the fire chief, waving his axe.

He marched straight into the house, and after a moment he brought out the smouldering television set and threw it on the compost heap at the bottom of the garden.

Within seconds, the whole place was swarming with fireman. One of them looked out of the lounge window.

'Luckily the woman unplugged the double sockets,' he said to his chief, 'otherwise the whole house might have burnt down.'

'The television set won't work again, that's for sure,' said the fire chief. 'Can you see any more damage in there?'

'The curtain's singed, this wooden table's blistered and there's a big hole in the carpet.' The fireman had a last look around. 'The whole place needs redecorating and tidying-up, but there's no futher risk of fire as far as I can see.'

Snowy heaved a sigh of relief.

'She was lucky to get off so lightly,' said the fire chief. 'Overloaded plugs are asking for trouble.' The fire chief put his axe back into his belt. 'Some people will never learn.'

'Can I have a ride on your fire engine?' asked Nobby.

'Not today, son, we're far too busy. The show's over now. You clear off home, like good boys.'

Nobby shrugged his shoulders, and he and Snowy wandered off.'

'Rotten sport,' grumbled Nobby. 'I hope he burns his toast.'

'I think we should go to your house,' said Snowy. 'Your face is covered with streaky polish.'

When the boys arrived at Nobby's house, they discovered that Mrs Hilton had recovered remarkably well. She had had a cup of tea, and was much less shaky after her ordeal. There was nothing wrong with the baby either, for she sat on the carpet, played with Nobby's toy cars, and gooed happily as soon as she saw the boys.

'Yeowh!' yelled Nobby at the baby. 'Who said you could play with my cars?'

'Goo!' said the baby.

'She's not hurting them,' said Mrs Clark. 'Now you go off and wash that dirty face of yours.'

Nobby almost choked. He picked up his best cars, as many as he could.

'Er . . . can I take your baby for a walk, Mrs Hilton?' he said. 'Aw, come on, Mum. She'd like to see the ducks. Wouldn't you like to see the ducksy wucksy, you goofy baby? Mrs Hilton, tell Mum it's all right to take your baby for a walk.'

Mrs Hilton put down her cup. 'That's a marvellous idea, if you would, boys. If you could take her off my hands for half an hour, that would give me a chance to tidy up the mess at home.'

'Good idea, Edna!' said Mrs Clark. 'I'll help you.'

Nobby gathered up the rest of his cars in a flash, while Mrs Hilton put her baby in the pram. Snowy and Nobby went off to take the baby for a walk.

'I thought this little monster would chew my cars to bits,' sighed Nobby, with relief. 'It took me hours to paint them. I just got her away from them in the nick of time.'

So the Cubs took the baby to the park, and

after Nobby got tired of chucking stones in the duck pond, they decided to come home. On the way home, however, the fire chief's car pulled up at the kerb beside them. The fire chief got out of his car.

'Well, boys,' he said cheerfully. 'I heard what really happened at the fire. I understand that you rang for us, unplugged the sockets from the mains, and rescued Mrs Hilton and her baby. Shake hands, boys,' he said. 'I'm proud to meet you. I wish everybody would behave as sensibly in an emergency.'

The embarrassed Cubs shook hands.

'It was Snowy's work,' said Nobby, modestly. 'Nobby did as much as I did.'

'And who opened the lounge window?' asked the fire chief.

'Snowy did,' said Nobby again, modestly.

The fire chief glared at Snowy. 'Well, don't do that again,' he said sternly. 'If you let the air get to a fire, it helps it to burn. You are lucky the TV set didn't burst into flames again.'

'I'm . . . I'm sorry,' said Snowy. 'I didn't know. Thank you for telling me.'

The fire chief grinned. 'Well, don't worry now. All told, you did very well in the circumstances. So after you've returned this young lady to her mother . . . if you would like to pop down to the fire-station, I'll arrange a special ride for you on our best fire-engine. I'll even get a couple of firemen's helmets for you to wear.'

'Really?' goggled Nobby.

'Sure I will. You did ask me for a ride, remember, and if there's time, I might even give you a lift on the hydraulic platform. See you at the fire-station. Come before six o'clock.'

The Cubs watched the fire-chief drive away, hardly believing they were not part of a dream.

'Yippee!' yelled Nobby, pushing the pram as fast as he could go. 'Wait until I tell the Cubs about this. They'll choke with envy.'

Suddenly Snowy laughed. He found the sight of Nobby so willingly pushing a pram unbelievably funny, for although Nobby was anxious to dump the baby in her mother's lap, and shoot off to the fire-station for a ride on a fire-engine, he had previously made it quite clear that he wouldn't be seen dead pushing a pram. He had wanted to get the baby away from his cars, true enough, but now that he had done that, Snowy could see no reason why he should now push the pram without the least sign of embarrassment.

'Pram-pusher!' he teased.

Nobby wiped a dirty hand over his polish-stained face. 'What does it matter now, Snowy? Nobody would recognise me behind this war-paint. Even my mother didn't recognise me when she saw me going to phone. She said, "Who do you think you are!" If Akela saw me now, he'd think I was someone different. Nobody would know this is me pushing a pram, unless I told them, and I certainly won't do that.'

Nobby walked on, pushing the pram on its way. 'The Cherokees are after me. They look mad . . .' he sang to the baby before him, 'but I'm not sad, for I'm singing a happy song.'

3

Odin replies

It didn't take the Scouts very long to raise the money they needed for their van. In fact, by Easter they had collected enough money to buy a fifteen-year-old meat van. It was a bit of an old crock, but it went (with a push-start). They cleaned it down. Nobby said it was more trouble to wash out that van than all the cars they had washed to collect the money to buy it. They painted it red and green, the Troop colours.

Money wasn't the only thing Cub Scouts were encouraged to collect. Collecting was a recognised Cub Scout hobby, and Akela said that the new Cubs should start a collection. Nobby and Snowy decided to make wild-flower collections. They spent a whole day in the woods and along the canal bank, and collected thirty-five different species. Snowy mounted his collection in a scrap-book and called to pick up Nobby to go to the Cubs' meeting. He rang Nobby's door-bell, and as he waited at the glass door he glanced through his scrap-book where he had mounted his collection. Snowy had neatly mounted and labelled his specimens, one to each page of his scrap-book, and he was anxious to see how Nobby's had turned out. Nobby opened the front door. He slid his woggle up his red and green neckerchief.

'Hi, Snowball.'

'Ready for Cubs?'

'Sure.' Nobby came out and slammed the front door behind him. 'Oh!' he said, scratching his ginger head. 'I've forgotten my lid.'

He rang the door-bell and, as it was not opened immediately, he opened the letter flap and shouted through. 'Hey, Mum, I've forgotten my lid.'

There was the sound of clumping feet and banging doors from within the house. It was his father's voice which answered from within.

'Do you think I've nothing better to do than open doors for you after you've locked yourself out?'

'I've only forgotten my lid,' shouted Nobby through the letter flap. 'If you poke it through the letter flap, you needn't open the door.'

Mr Clark opened the front door, hit Nobby over the head with his Cub cap and closed the door again.

'Thanks, Dad,' said Nobby.

'And good-bye to you,' came Mr Clark's voice from within. 'I'll be glad when that boy's married.'

'Hey, Nobby,' said Snowy, pulling Nobby's arm. 'You've forgotten your wild flowers. Don't you want to show Akela your collection?'

Nobby shrugged himself free and walked on reluctantly towards the Cub Scout hut. 'I haven't any wild flowers,' he grunted. 'I . . .'

'But . . . but we collected them together. We both collected the same. We spent a whole day collecting them.'

'I put my wild flowers in a jam jar to keep them fresh, but they wilted in the morning sunshine and Mum threw them in the dustbin.'

'Oh, no, Nobby! You are the end. Where do you think you'll get another collection before Cubs tonight? Last night's thunderstorm will have ruined any that are left. You won't be able to make a decent collection until next year.'

Nobby hunched his shoulders, but he still walked on. Suddenly he snapped his fingers. 'I know, I'll collect some rocks.' He grinned. 'You can use rocks for a collection. There're plenty on the gravel path all around headquarters. Come on, Snowy, let's hurry. There's just time to make a collection before Cubs start.'

At Cubs, Snowy showed Akela his wild flower collection. In fact, Akela was so pleased with it that he told Snowy to put the collection on the display table so that everyone could see it. Snowy put his scrap-book beneath the polished board on which were painted in gold the Cub Scout Promise and the Cub Scout Law.

'And what have you got, Nobby?' asked Akela.

Nobby grinned and put a handful of pebbles on the table.

'What's ... what's that?' asked Akela blankly.

'Rocks,' grinned Nobby. 'I collected a few rocks.'

'But ... but these are all the same. For a collection, you have to have a set of different objects in the same series. If you were collecting rocks, for example, you should collect pieces of limestone, granite, sandstone, lava, coral and so on.'

'These are all different,' said Nobby.

'What's different about them?'

'Well . . . there're round ones.'

'Yes. I can see that.'

'And little egg-shaped ones.'

'Yes?'

'And circular ones, and spherical ones, and oval-shaped ones,' said Nobby, 'and there's a little flat shiny one.'

'That "little flat shiny one" is a drawing pin stuck in my table,' said Akela. He groaned. 'This collection is hopeless, lad. I don't know how you have the nerve to bring such rubbish in here. It's no more than a handful of dirty pebbles, which you could have picked up outside headquarters.'

'Is it any good?' asked Nobby eagerly.

'No, it is not,' said Akela firmly. He blew a long blast on his whistle to attract the attention of all the Cubs. 'Cubs,' he said. 'This week-end we'll have a Pack outing to the beach. I'm going to show little Nobby Clark how to set about making a collection. If any of you want to collect geological specimens. . . .'

'Pardon?' said Nobby.

'Rocks to you. I'll show you where and how to find them. Listen, lads,' went on Akela, 'we are going to the beach on Sunday. I want to show all of you, particularly little Nobby here, how to go about collecting rocks.'

'Yippee!' yelled the Cubs. 'Good old Nobby.'

So, on the following Sunday morning, the red and green van set off, crammed with a dozen chattering Cubs. They were off to the seaside for the day. Even the meaty pong, which still clung to the van in spite of the thorough washing, did not put them off. The Cubs were excited. When they arrived at the beach, they charged out of the van like a pack of yelping foxhounds.

Akela caught Nobby by the tail of his jersey before he rushed off with the others to have a little dig in the sand.

'Now, now, little Nobby Clark,' he said firmly, 'we came here for a purpose. I want you to start collecting as many *different* types of stone as you can. . . .'

'But. . . but. . . but. . . I want to have a dig.'

'Never mind digging for the moment. You are here to collect stones. As soon as I've set up camp, I'll join you and show you just what to collect. Until then, see what you can collect yourself, but remember to keep out of the water at all costs. Do you understand.'

'Yes, yes,' said Nobby excitedly. 'Then after

that, will I be able to have a little play before we go home?'

'Yes, you can have your little play. Now be off with you.'

'I'll help, Nobby,' said Snowy. 'Come on. We'll soon collect all the stones you need.'

Snowy and Nobby charged over the shingle.

'Cor, there're about eight hundred and twenty-seven million tons of rocks here,' said Nobby. 'How many do I have to collect?'

'As many different types as you can find,' suggested Snowy. 'Ah, here's a good one. It's got a blue and green line running through it. It's called an agate.'

'I've got a bit here you can see through,' said Nobby.

'That's a bit of sea-washed glass!' said Snowy.

Nobby threw away his bit of sea-washed glass, but he collected quite an interesting set of stones — agates of many patterns, a piece of amber, even a piece of jet, besides many other coloured stones which they could not, at that moment, identify. Nobby loaded the stones in his pockets.

'Thanks, Snowy. I'm about two tons heavier now.'

Snowy took a deep breath of the cold fresh air. The sea was misty, and it was not possible to see far, but the air was bracing. It was a pleasure to be alive.

'Race you to the water's edge and back, Nobby,' challenged Snowy.

'Right-ho!' said Nobby, in a flash.

Snowy sprinted away, shot past Nobby and raced across the long beach to the sea.

'Wait for me, Snowy,' wailed Nobby helplessly.

Snowy did not slacken his pace, for he knew Nobby was a swift runner, and would never forgive him if he did not run his best. As Snowy ran, the mist seemed to recede before him, and he saw the long waves sliding in towards the beach and the swell beyond. He ran a long way before he reached the water's edge.

Eventually Nobby, walking like a lame duck, caught up.

'Phew!' said Nobby, panting violently. 'That race was not fair. Why didn't you wait for me? I couldn't run with my pockets full of stones. Every step I took, I thought my pants would fall down.'

'Sorry, Nobby. I thought you wanted me to give you a good race.'

The Cubs ambled along the water's edge. They could not see any of their Cubs party back on the beach, for the camp seemed to be enveloped in the distant mist.

'You've got a collection good enough for your Silver Arrow tests now, Nobby – that is if your mother doesn't throw them in the dustbin.'

'First, I have to get my Bronze Arrow, Snowy,' said Nobby. 'I'm not Snowy White. I haven't passed any Arrow tests yet, and I don't think I ever shall.'

'You'll pass easily enough,' said Snowy confidently.

Snowy looked about him. The mist seemed to be quite thick now, especially over the sea; but of course, as they walked on, the mist receded before them at the same rate as it closed in behind.

'We'd better head back to camp now, Nobby. We can't see the Cubs from here. I wouldn't like to be caught in this mist.'

'Okay, Snowy, but I'm not racing you back with these stones in my pocket. After I've shown them to Akela I'll show you how to run. I'll give you ten paces start and still beat you in a hundred.'

'Okay, Nobby, you're on.'

The Cubs turned away from the water's edge,

41

but as is common in those parts, patches of fog were created out of the mist. They came in from the sea, sometimes as quickly as the tide comes in over a flat beach. Snowy and Nobby walked straight into one such patch, which enveloped them before they were aware of it. They found they could only see about thirty paces ahead. They hurried away, then for some strange reason, they found themselves back at the water's edge.

'We must have gone round in circles,' said Snowy light-heartedly. 'Pity, we don't have a compass with us. We could use one now. I intend to get one just as soon as I get home.'

The Cubs doubled back, but before long they were again at the water's edge. They wandered around for a while, trying to get their bearings.

'We went round in circles again,' chuckled Nobby.

'I'm sure we didn't.' Snowy was uneasy now.

Again they tried to find their way through the fog, but again, after only a few paces, they came up to the water's edge.

'We must be surrounded by water,' said Nobby jokingly.

'Listen,' said Snowy. 'I think you may be right.'

They listened, and heard the water lapping around them on all sides. Indeed, as Nobby had suggested, they seemed to be completely surrounded by water. The fog had thickened too, and now they could see no more than a few paces ahead.

'I . . . I hate to say this, Nobby, but I think we're trapped on a sandbank. We . . . we're probably cut off from the beach. That means we . . . we'll have to wade through the water to reach the beach. Akela said we had to keep out of the water, but there's nothing else we can do.'

Nobby slipped off his shoes and tied them round his neck by the laces. He wiggled his toes in the fresh air.

'A little wade won't do us any harm, Snowy,' he said. 'Hey, don't toes look funny? My dad says they don't look half as funny as my face, but I think they do.'

'Never mind funny faces now,' said Snowy. 'We'll have to think pretty quickly about getting ourselves off this sandbank before we're caught in the tide. The problem is, which way should we go? We can't see far in this fog bank. We should go to the west, I know that. But which way is west?'

Nobby pondered for a moment. 'If we find a tree with moss growing on one side, that's the north side, and west is on the left-hand side. Even I know that.'

'You won't find trees growing on beaches,' said Snowy impatiently.

'Well, when the stars come out, all we have to do is find the Pole Star which is in the north. The Pole Star is easy to find. All you have to do is look for the seven stars in the Plough. . . .'

'We'll be caught in the tide, swept away and drowned before the stars come out, even if you could see the stars in a fog, which you can't,' said Snowy. 'Oh, I wish I'd thought about carrying an emergency compass before now.'

Nobby spat on to the palm of his hand, then slapped his finger on his palm to splash out the moisture which hit him in the eye.

'That's north,' he said, pointing over his shoulder. 'We should go that-a-way.'

'That's an odd way to work out directions. I don't believe for a moment that you're right.' Snowy was confused. 'I can't suggest anything better and I suppose your way is as good as any. Let's try it anyway.'

'Okay, Snowy, I'll lead the way.'

The Cubs walked to the water's edge, but Snowy was uneasy. He had second thoughts about going on so blindly.

'We . . . we can't risk it, Nobby. If . . . if this is not the right way, we'll walk into the sea. We've got to be certain of our direction, and we've got to sort ourselves out very quickly or we'll be in real trouble.'

Nobby hesitated at the water's edge. He noticed Snowy looking about him anxiously in all directions. 'It's not that bad, Snowy.'

'I wish I had your confidence,' laughed Snowy hollowly. He knew they were in serious trouble, but he found comfort in Nobby's presence. They were both in the same mess together. 'We'll have to shout for help, Nobby.'

44

'Help!' yelled Nobby. 'Help, help. I need somebody.'

'Together,' said Snowy.

'Help, help, help!' they yelled together, as loudly as they could.

'Help! We're trapped on a sandbank.'

Snowy sighed. 'It's no good, Nobby. No one can hear us at this distance above the noise of the waves. The camp is 500 metres away. We'll just have to take a chance. If we stay here we'll drown, so we have nothing to lose by. . . .'

'Anything you say, Snowy. I don't mind.'

The Cubs walked to the water's edge. Again Snowy had his doubts.

'We can't go on, it's too risky, Nobby.' Then suddenly Snowy brightened. 'Keep quiet, I've got an idea.' He cupped his hands to his mouth. 'Odin!' he called out to the fog. He listened carefully to the swirling fog, then he turned to one side. He took a deep breath. 'Odin!' he called again. Again he turned. 'Odin!' But the only reply he got was that of his own echo. 'We go this way,' said Snowy confidently.

Nobby shrugged his shoulders. 'If you say so,' he said doubtfully. 'It all looks the same to me, but I suppose it's better than staying here.'

The Cubs turned back. When they came to the water's edge Snowy slipped off his shoes and socks, stuffed them down his belt and waded into the water. After a few paces, the water came up to his knees.

'The water's very deep,' he said. 'We may

have to swim, but we've got to risk it before it's too late. I'm sure this is the right direction.'

'I hope you're right. I . . . I can't swim,' said Nobby, wading in after Snowy.

This was the first time Snowy had detected a trace of anxiety in Nobby's voice.

'Hold on to me,' said Snowy, holding out his hand. 'I'll help you.'

'I can float,' said Nobby bravely.

Nobby put his hand on Snowy's shoulder as they waded deeper and deeper into the water. Periodically Snowy called out ahead. He waded on, leading the way. At one stage the swell brought the water up to their waists. It was a frightening experience, with the water so deep and the fog all around, but still they waded on. Eventually the sand sloped up and the water

level dropped. They felt themselves rising out of the water at every step.

'Good old Snowy!' yelled Nobby excitedly. 'You've got us back on the beach. How did you do it?'

46

'We're not out of trouble yet.' Snowy cupped his hands to his mouth. 'Odin!' he called again.

'White! Clark!' came a voice out of the fog. It was Akela. 'Where are you?'

'Here, here,' answered the Cubs.

Nobby and Snowy squelched out of the water. They were wet through from the waists down, but they did not care. Akela appeared out of the fog to meet them.

'Where have you been?' he asked angrily. 'I heard you shout. I thought I told you to stay out of the water?'

'We were trapped on a sandbank,' explained Snowy.

'Snowy found the way back to the beach in all this fog. Snowy led the way.'

'You are a couple of young idiots. You could have easily drowned, don't you see? Come on, back to the van. We'll have to get you out of your wet clothes before you catch your death of cold.' Akela took the boys firmly by the hands and walked them quickly up the beach. 'Don't you listen to anything I say?' went on Akela firmly. 'If I was your father, I'd give you a good hiding, both of you. You're lucky you didn't lose your sense of direction in this fog.'

'I did,' said Nobby modestly, 'but Snowy knew exactly where we were going. All he did was call "Oh, din", and he knew just which way to go.'

'Oh, din?' repeated Akela. 'What are you talking about?'

'I once read a book about the Vikings who used to sail in these parts,' explained Snowy. 'When they were caught in a fog, or at night, they used to call out "Odin", the name of their god. When they heard their echo bounce back from the shore, they knew where the shore was so they could avoid running aground. They could sail right up the middle of a river on the blackest of nights by using their voices as bats do, like radar.'

'Very clever, very clever,' said Akela, not at all amused. 'Now get your towels from the van, give yourselves a good rub down and put on your dry bathing trunks. If you wander away more than five paces from me, I'll lock you both up in the van until I get you home.'

Snowy and Nobby dried themselves and changed, and Akela drove the Pack home in the van.

'This rotten fog has spoilt our Pack outing,' moaned one little Cub, as the van lurched away through the seaside town. 'We had just buried our Sixer in the sand up to his neck when we had to come away in this stinky van. It was a waste of time coming.'

'At least Nobby doesn't think so,' said Snowy, wrapping the blanket around his legs. 'He's got a super collection of stones to show you and Akela, haven't you, Nobby? Show us your stones, Nobby.'

Nobby gulped and slunk into his blanket. 'I . . . I haven't got any,' he said faintly.

'What?' groaned Snowy. 'What . . . what did you do with them?'

'When we were up to our waists in the water,' Nobby confessed, 'I . . . I dumped the stones so they wouldn't make me sink.'

'Oh, no,' groaned Snowy. 'That could only happen to you. How . . . what can you collect now? How will you . . .?'

'I suppose I'll have to collect what Mum suggested in the first place.'

'What's that?' asked Snowy.

'Buttons,' mumbled Nobby softly, so no one could hear him.

4

Birdbrain's birdbox

Nobby Clark was disappointed that he did not do very well as a collector but not unduly so, for there were many more activities in the Cub programme, and Akela had particularly asked his Cubs to bring along a handcraft sample to the next meeting. Nobby had borrowed his father's tools, when his father was not looking, and built himself what he considered to be a superb letter-box. It didn't turn out too badly, and Nobby proudly took it to Cubs to show Akela.

Akela looked over Nobby's head. 'Quiet, lads. Listen to me. It's such a lovely evening that I have decided to take you outside for the first hour. Now, what shall we do?'

'I've . . . I've . . . I've got something I've made for my Bronze Arrow,' piped up little Nobby, tugging Akela's sleeve. 'It's handcraft. . . .'

'Patience, patience, patience, it's not hand-craft time yet,' said Akela, with no more than a glance at Nobby's box. 'It's not going to blow up within the next five minutes, is it? You must learn to wait. It's outdoor activities now. I'll look at your model later.'

'But ... but ... but ...' said Nobby. 'I've got a beautiful letter-box here.'

'Put it on the table and I'll examine it later.' Akela looked over Nobby's head towards Snowy, who was holding a one-metre wide kite he had made with a spruce frame covered with doped linen.

'What have you got there, Snowy? Do you want to fly it when we go outside?'

Snowy noticed that his pal, Nobby, was on the point of bursting into tears. Snowy put the kite behind his back.

'No, no,' he said. 'I've got nothing to show you tonight.'

'Didn't you bring your kite to fly this evening?'

'No, no, no,' said Snowy. 'I just brought it along to show the Cubs. Have you seen Nobby's super letter-box? It's the best I've ever seen. It ... it makes my effort look a bit amateurish.'

'Yes, yes,' said Nobby, brightening up. He held out his letter-box. 'I ... I ... I made it. I'm going to screw it to our front gate-post. It will save the postman walking up the drive. I think I'll make letter-boxes for everyone in the neighbourhood. They will save the postman wearing out his big boots.'

'All right, all right, Nobby, let me see it.' Akela sat down.

Nobby gave him his letter-box. It was made

with plywood sheets firmly screwed and glued, and painted in bright, pillar-box red. A big black arrow pointed to the little rectangular opening in the front, and white painted words read 'Put your post in hear'. But the words were so large that to read the complete sentence you had to look at the front, side, back, side and bottom of the letter-box, in that order.

'Put post in your hear,' read Akela, looking at all sides of the box.

'No, no, no,' said Nobby. 'You've read it wrong. You should read the side before you read the back. It says "Put your post in hear". See?'

Akela groaned. Ignoring for the moment the matter of Nobby's spelling, he pointed to the little rectangular opening in the front of the letter-box. 'But you've only got a little letter-opening. What . . . what if you have a wide letter?'

'Put it in sideways,' replied Nobby quickly.

'But what if it's long and wide, say quarto size?'

'Quarto, quarto, what's a quarto? Is that the same as two pintos?'

Akela held up his Cub register, which was the size of a school exercise book. 'This is the old quarto size,' he said. 'Suppose the postman had a letter this size. How would he get it through that little rectangular opening into your letter-box?'

'Easy,' said Nobby, grinning. 'All he has to do is bend it and squeeze it through the little hole.'

'But you can't bend, say, photographs.'

'Photographs,' said Nobby.

'Well, can you?'

'Well you could if you bend them carefully into a little circle, like a scroll. But you can still put little letters in. I'll show you.' Nobby picked up Akela's Cub register and waved it in front of his Cub Scout leader's face. 'Imagine this is a letter, eh? I'm a postman, eh?' Nobby pretended to open an invisible gate. He waltzed up an imaginary path and knocked on the top of his letter-box. 'Knock, knock, anyone in?' Then before anyone could stop him, he folded up Akela's register and popped it through the little rectangular opening.

For that performance, Akela should have immediately recommended him for the Actor of the Year Award; instead, Akela shook the box. His register rattled inside. He looked at the back of the box.

'How do I get it out?'

'From the back,' said Nobby. 'I'll show you.' He looked at the back of his letter-box. 'Oh!'

'Oh?'

'I've . . . I've forgotten to make a back door. I've . . . I've screwed up the back.'

'Well, how can I get my register?'

'You'll have to get it out of the little hole in the front.'

'How can I do that?'

'Well, you know how to get coins out of a money box with a knife, don't you? All you have to do is to get a big knife, about 100 millimetres wide, pop it through this little hole, turn the letter-box upside down, and the register will slide out.'

'You can't turn a letter-box upside down if it's screwed to a gate-post.' Akela threw the box at Nobby. 'Get my register out of that box in half an hour, otherwise I'll come along with a sledge-hammer to use on your head.'

Akela walked to the door. 'Okay, Cubs, outside for games. Everyone else outside.'

The Cubs barged through the heavy swing door. Each Cub, as he barged through, was in such a hurry that he let the door fly back and thump the Cub behind. Thirty Cubs charged through the door. Twenty-nine of them were thumped by the door. Nobby, however, did not take much notice. He looked at his letter-box.

'He's only joking, Nobby,' said Snowy. 'He hasn't got a sledge-hammer, and even if he had, he wouldn't use it on your head.'

54

'He might do worse than that,' said Nobby glumly. 'He might smash up my letter-box.'

Akela looked back from the door. 'Hurry up, Snowy. Let's have a go with your kite.'

Snowy sensed that Nobby was envious of him for having the kite.

'I . . . I . . . I only bought it to show the Cubs, Nobby,' said Snowy, trying not to embarrass his friend. 'Honest!'

'I don't mind,' said Nobby.

'Never mind about that now,' shouted Akela from the door. 'Bring your kite outside, Snowy. You stay here, Nobby, you menace, until you've got my register out of that thieving little box of yours.'

Snowy shrugged his shoulders, tucked his kite under his arm and walked out, as Akela held the door open for him. Outside, the Cubs crowded round him.

'I wish I could make a kite like that,' said one envious Cub.

Snowy looked about him. It was a calm, still evening, perfect for flying model aircraft, but not at all suitable for kite flying. In a way, Snowy was pleased, for tonight of all nights, he did not want to impress Akela, not when his pal, Nobby, was not very popular. Snowy gave the end of his tow-line to his Sixer to hold, and walked away with the kite to take the slack out of the tow-line. He held up his kite, and released it. There was not a breath of wind in the sky. The kite slid to the ground.

'It's too heavy,' said Snowy modestly. 'It won't fly.'

'Not enough wind,' said Akela. 'All right, Snowy, take it inside, and come out again to join our games. The rest of you Cubs form two lines – move!'

The mob of Cubs scrambled to sort themselves out. Snowy walked into the building, quite relieved that his kite had not flown.

He found Nobby sitting cross-legged on the floor, pulling the cover of Akela's Cub register out of his letter-box. A pile of torn, crumpled pages littered the floor around him.

'Hi, Snowy,' he said. 'I've nearly got Akela's book out of the box. It's a bit torn, but the only way I could get it out was by pulling out the pages a bit at a time.'

Snowy groaned. 'And what do you think Akela will say to that?'

'Oh, he won't mind,' grinned Nobby. 'Akela is a good Cub Scout Leader, one of the best. He won't mind. He can easily stick the pages together again.' Nobby pulled the last bit of the register from the box, and crumpled all the pieces in his hands. He picked up his precious letter-box and an old metal name-plate he had been using to poke the register through the opening. 'Come on, Snowy. Let's go outside and join in the games.'

Nobby dashed to the heavy swing door, but just as he reached it, the door was pushed open from the other side and hit Nobby right on the end of his nose. He yelled out in agony, and as he fell backwards he threw up his arms and scattered the torn pages of the register about him like confetti. The box went on one side of the room, the metal name-plate on the other. Nobby sat on the floor and rubbed his nose. Akela came through the door and stood before him.

'Sorry, Nobby,' said Akela apologetically. 'I didn't know you were behind the door.' Then Akela noticed the torn pages of his register lying on the floor. He gulped, choked, grew red in the face, then blue. He spluttered, then found his voice. 'What's this?' he bellowed

Nobby rubbed his nose. 'It's your register. I got it out of the little opening.'

'You . . .' Akela lost his voice again. He tried to control himself, with difficulty.

'You didn't half give me a whack on the nose,' said Nobby, still sitting on the floor and rubbing his nose. 'My nose is flat enough. I don't want it pushing inside out.'

Akela turned away to hide his smile. He had recovered himself.

'I'm sorry, Nobby. It was an accident, believe me. Get outside and join in the Cub games.'

'Goodie, goodie,' said Nobby. He jumped up and, leaving his belongings where they had fallen, he charged through the swing door, which had so recently nearly knocked him for six.

Akela walked across the hall to get his whistle from his coat pocket. He looked back at Snowy picking up the torn pages of the Cub register.

'One of these days I'll hoist that little monkey up the flag pole by his skinny neck,' Akela muttered to himself. 'That boy can't do a thing right. Now where did I put that whistle?'

Snowy picked up the pieces of register, arranged them in some sort of order and put them on the table, then he was ready to go out to join in the Cub games. He approached the swing door carefully, for he did not want to be hit in the face. Normally the door was held open by a metal block, but somebody had taken it away. Suddenly Snowy noticed the flat piece of metal which Nobby had used to poke the register out of his letter-box. It was an old name-plate which had originally been used by the Scouts, before they had rearranged their quarters. Snowy picked up the flat plate. It was quite thin and he easily bent it into a V-shape and used it as a wedge to keep open the door.

'That's very clever,' said Akela, coming through the open door. 'Blow me down. Why didn't I think of that? Very clever indeed.' Akela chuckled to himself. 'You are full of bright ideas, aren't you?'

Snowy avoided his eyes, and was relieved that neither Nobby nor any of the Cubs was around to hear Akela's praise.

Akela blew his whistle to call the Cubs to order. He organised a leap-frog game, in which, Snowy was relieved to see, Nobby joined whole-heartedly. Nobby had forgotten all about his thumped nose, in fact he was on top form. He croaked like a bullfrog before he jumped, even if he didn't jump like one. He jumped more like a goat. He certainly butted a few Cubs who had bent down for his benefit.

It was a beautiful summer evening. The Cubs all enjoyed themselves, and afterwards Nobby was happy enough as he and Snowy walked home. Snowy looked at the letter-box which Nobby carried under his arm.

'What are you going to do with your letter-box now, Nobby?' he asked. 'Can't you make a door in the back?'

Nobby held his box in front of him so he could admire it. 'It's a good box, isn't it, Snowy? I'm going to put it in the sycamore tree so that the birds can use it for a bird-house. There are some swifts in our eaves this year. Perhaps they'll want to use it.'

Nobby thought for a moment. 'I'll take my box back to Akela when the birds have finished with it. Akela's fair, isn't he? If the birds prove my box is useful, maybe he'll look at it again . . . for my Bronze Arrow.'

Snowy nodded firmly. 'He'll pass you, Nobby. If the birds don't fail you, Akela won't.'

5

Disguise in focus

Making collections and handcraft work were very interesting, but what really fascinated Snowy was photography. The Cubs had a photographer's badge, which would be awarded to a Cub who could show twelve suitable photographs which he had taken himself, and Snowy had set his heart on winning that badge. When he got a little camera for his ninth birthday, Snowy immediately set about taking his photographs. He got his father, who was a chemist, to develop the negatives and make him a set of prints. He invited Nobby in to see them.

Snowy put four corners on a photograph and mounted it neatly in his album. He closed his

album and with a soft pencil wrote the lettering on the front cover.

2nd BILLINGTON CUB SCOUT PACK
G. WHITE – TAWNY SIX

Nobby Clark, with mouth open and eyes goggling, watched him work. When Snowy was satisfied that he had the lettering spaced correctly, he inked it with a colouring pen.

'There you are, Nobby,' he said, finishing off his work, 'that's the last of my twelve photographs.' He showed his album to Nobby. 'I took all those pictures in the park during one evening. There's a picture of a pup, remember Poggles? There's a picture of a cypress tree, another of two children playing, one of the war memorial. . . .'

Nobby looked at the pictures enviously. 'Why, these are super, just like real photographs.' He licked his lips as if he was hungry and about to eat the album. 'You're sure to get your photographer's badge, Snowy, now you've got your Bronze Arrow.'

'I hope so,' said Snowy, putting away his album in his desk drawer.

'I wish I could take photographs,' said Nobby. 'I did try once, as a matter of fact. I tried to take a picture of Mum in the kitchen, but she didn't like it.'

'Why not? Were you using a trick water-squirting camera?'

'Oh, no. It was a real camera, in fact it was Dad's best camera, but I dropped it in Mum's flour bowl. You should have heard her shout.'

'You can take some more photographs. It's easy, really.'

'Oh, Dad won't let me use his camera any more. He says if he wants his camera smashing up, he'll jump on it himself.'

'You can borrow my camera any time you want. It's not very good – it only has a plastic lens – but it works, and it has a film in it.'

'Oh, thanks, Snowy,' said Nobby excitedly. 'I've only got fifteen pence, but you can take it as part payment for the film. I'll pay you the rest when I can. I'll tell Dad I owe you some money for a film so he won't stop my pocket-money for a few weeks. Go on, Snowy, take the money, please.'

Snowy smiled. 'All right, Nobby.' He took the money and handed over the camera. 'Here's the camera. The film's inside, and it's all yours.'

'You're a pal. Do you think I can really get a Cub's badge when I've got my Bronze Arrow?'

'Why not? I'll show you what to do. If you press that little button, you can take a picture. I'll just tell Mum we're off to the park.'

'You're a pal, Snowy, a real pal. I'll pay you back for the film of course. I'll pay you before I pay for Mum's broken flour bowl.'

So the two Cubs wandered off to the local park. Nobby was delighted with the camera. He kept pointing it at everyone he saw and took peeps at them through the view-finder. He found it sheer agony keeping his itchy little finger off the button.

'I'd like to be a photographer when I grow up,' said Nobby, 'but Dad says if I touch his camera again, he won't let me grow up.'

'He'll change his mind when you show him your pictures,' said Snowy. They were inside the park gates by this time. Snowy looked about him. 'I'll stand on my head here, Nobby, and you can take a photograph of me, eh? Unusual photographs are better than posed photographs. All you have to do is to point the camera at me, frame me in the view-finder and press the shutter-release button, right? The first unused frame is already set up. I'll take off the lens cover to expose the lens, there. Since I'll be about three metres away, we can set the focus at three metres, so I'll be in sharp focus. The background shrubs will come out slightly blurred, but that doesn't matter. All right, Nobby?'

'You do know a lot about photography, Snowy.'

'I'll stand on my head here.'

Snowy stood about three metres from the camera, knelt down and stood on his head.

'Ready when you are, Nobby,' said Snowy, wobbling a little on his head. 'Point the camera at me.'

Nobby raised the camera and peered through the view-finder. 'Yoo-hoo, I can see you.'

'Move your thumb,' said Snowy, struggling to

keep his balance. 'It's covering the lens. You don't want to take a photograph of your thumb, do you?'

'Oh, no, sorry.' Nobby moved his thumb.

'Press the button, Nobby,' said Snowy. 'Hurry up, I can't stand on my head much longer.'

'I can't see where the button is,' muttered Nobby, 'not when I'm looking through the view-finder at the same time. Just a minute. I'll use one eye through the view-finder and another for the camera release button.'

'Feel for it,' gasped Snowy, wobbling violently. 'Hurry up, hurry up.'

'I've pressed the wrong button,' said Nobby.

'Let me show you again,' said Snowy. As he lowered his feet to the ground he heard the camera click. 'What are you doing?'

'I've taken your picture.'

'You've what? I wasn't ready.'

'Well, I still got you. It may turn out all right. It may not be a picture of you standing on your head, but it will be a good picture of you with your bottom stuck up in the air.'

'Why did you want to take me like that?'

'Ah well, we've got plenty of film left. I can take another picture of you standing on your head.'

'Don't bother,' said Snowy, walking away. 'We'll find something else.'

As the Cubs wandered around the park, Snowy suggested that Nobby should take a photograph of a picturesque old oak tree leaning over at an odd angle. Nobby took the picture, with Snowy apparently holding up the leaning tree with one hand, and even Snowy had to admit that it should come out all right. They then took a picture of a swan gliding across the pond trailing a ripple in the calm waters, and of the humped-back stone bridge over the stream, a long-distance shot of the tropical plant conservatory, a fountain spraying water into a goldfish pond, the tulip beds in full bloom, and a little boy feeding the ducks.

Nobby was delighted with his work. It seemed that, now that he had overcome his initial clumsiness, he was a natural photographer. He had a flair for seeing the right subject from the best angle. He avoided direct sunlight, and chose subjects that were gently formed in light and shade. He kept his camera steady, held his breath and operated his shutter smoothly. He judged the focal distance like a practised expert. Clumsy Nobby was no more. At last he had discovered his true art.

So Nobby took enough photographs to prove he was becoming a competent photographer. He still had a couple of unexposed frames left, and as they were making their way home Nobby looked for another subject so that the whole film would be ready to develop and print. He saw a tramp on a park bench, airing his toes and eating a cheese sandwich. Nobby aimed his camera.

'Dis guy's in focus,' he said. 'Say cheese and wiggle your toes.'

The tramp spluttered out a bit of his cheese sandwich. 'Don't take my picture,' he roared, but it was too late. Nobby had already pressed the trigger.

The tramp jumped up, threw away his cheese sandwich and lunged at Nobby. 'Gimme that camera, you little wretch,' he yelled.

Nobby yelped and leapt back out of reach. Then the tramp came at him again, and Nobby sped away like a frightened little rabbit, just out of reach of the outstretched hand. He was

nearly caught, for the tramp was very deter-
mined not to let him get away. However, the
tramp was handicapped by his bare feet,
particularly as the path was gravel covered. He
gave up the chase when he stood on a sharp
chipping, and limped back to his seat to pull on
his boots.

'If you don't give me that film, I'll skin you
alive,' he threatened. 'I didn't say you could
take my photo.'

'I was only taking a picture of the empty seat,'
said Nobby. 'I didn't ask you to sit there.'

The Cubs watched the tramp as he pulled on
his boots.

'You've forgotten to put on your socks,' said
Nobby.

The tramp growled angrily, and as soon as he
had slipped his feet into his boots he jumped up
and charged at them. Nobby fled. Snowy stood
his ground, for he did not like running away
from danger. But the tramp was not interested
in Snowy. He pushed Snowy aside and went
after Nobby.

Fortunately Lady Luck was on Nobby's side,
for the tramp, in his hurry to catch Nobby, had
not only omitted to put on his socks, but had
not tied up the string he was using for boot-
laces. He clanked along after Nobby as fast as
he could. He chased him round a tree, round
the shrubs, round the park bench and round
and round the tree again. When Nobby came
round the park bench for the third time, Snowy

fell in with him, and together they ran along the path. They increased their lead to about thirty metres by the time they shot through the park gates. As it happened, at that time, a bus was waiting at the bus stop. Nobby glanced back and saw the tramp closing up fast.

'Quick, Snowy, on the bus,' he shrieked.

Nobby leapt on the bus like a squirrel going into its hole. Snowy climbed up after him.

'Two halves,' said Nobby to the driver/conductor. 'He'll pay.' He pointed at Snowy. 'He's got fifteen pence.'

Snowy paid up and collected the tickets. He went to join Nobby on the back seat of the bus, but instead of driving off, the driver waited for the old tramp who was running up, waving his hands as though conducting a great symphony orchestra. The tramp climbed on to the bus and paid his fare from a roll of five-pound notes. Snowy and Nobby got up and left via the rear emergency exit. As soon as they stepped on the ground, the bus drove away, taking their pursuer with it. They could see the old tramp on the back seat, waving his fist at them. Nobby raised his camera and took his last picture of the back of the bus.

'What's up with him?' said Snowy, wondering why the tramp should be so upset about them.

'I suppose he's just ashamed of his ugly face,' muttered Nobby, 'and he doesn't want to leave his picture to posterity.'

The Cubs wandered home. 'I suppose we should tell our parents about this, Nobby,' said Snowy. 'I don't like worrying them, but it's something they ought to know. They'd be annoyed if they found we were keeping it secret.'

'I don't know about that,' said Nobby. 'When I told Dad that the park-keeper had chased me last year and had given me a good whack with his stick, Dad gave me another whack to make sure I wouldn't forget the first. Sometimes I think all the grown-ups in this world are ganged up against poor little me.'

'Come home with me, Nobby. I'll ask Dad when he comes in to print your pictures tonight.'

'You will? Good-oh! Thanks, Snowy.'

So the Cubs went back to Snowy's home. Snowy casually mentioned to his mother what had happened to them in the park, but he was very surprised at her reaction – she almost had hysterics. She immediately telephoned the police. She wailed and ranted. She told the boys that they had had a very lucky escape. She told them they might have been abducted. She said they might never have seen their families again.

The Cubs were glad to get away from her and go up to Snowy's room.

'She does go on,' said Nobby. 'Is she always like that?'

'She flaps a bit at times.'

'My mum flaps a bit at me too, but she'd say

nobody with any sense would ever want to kidnap me, and if they did, they'd pretty soon be glad to bring me back.'

The boys expected to be left to play alone in Snowy's room in peace until Mr White came home, but it was not to be. Within minutes, the police arrived and two constables came up to Snowy's room.

'You say you were chased by a man?' said one of the policemen.

Snowy nodded.

'Can you describe him?'

'Oh, he was about your height, with black hair,' said Snowy. 'And he was ugly. He had a flat face, a squint in his eye, and a pimple on his nose.'

'A pimple on his nose?' repeated the policeman.

'Yeah! As a matter of fact,' said Nobby nonchalantly, 'I've got a picture of him in this camera.'

Before anyone could stop him, Nobby opened the back of the camera and pulled out the strip of film and held it up to the light. Snowy groaned and collapsed on his bed.

'Oh, Nobby, you've exposed the film before it was developed. It's spoilt!'

'Oh? Oh!'

The policeman was also visibly disappointed. He breathed deeply to control himself.

'Mrs White,' he said, 'do you happen to have any old newspapers? It's Monday evening's I'm interested in.'

71

'I have a pile of newspapers in the shed,' said Mrs White. 'I'll see what I've got. I'll get them for you.'

Mrs White left the room. The police constable took Nobby by the shoulders.

'You're not going to lock me up, are you?' croaked Nobby.

'No, no, son. Just tell me again. Did you say this man had a pimple on his nose?'

'A great big pimple,' said Nobby, squeezing his own nose, 'so big that I couldn't say for sure which was his nose and which was the pimple.'

'And he wore a moustache and beard?'

'Yes,' said Snowy, 'about two weeks' growth.'

Mrs White came in with a pile of newspapers.

'I've got about six months' supply of newspapers here,' she said. 'I keep meaning to give them to the dustman, but he's in and out and away before I've had time to catch him. I suppose I'll have to keep them until he comes round for his Christmas-box.'

'Quite, quite,' said the policeman, not at all interested in what she was saying. He glanced through the pile of papers, took out one and spread it on Snowy's desk. The policeman pointed to a photograph on the front page of the newspaper. 'Would you say your tramp looks anything like that man, for instance.'

'No, no, definitely not,' said Nobby firmly. 'That man hasn't got a beard for a start. This tramp was ugly, like The Monster from Five Thousand Fathoms.'

Snowy glanced at the newspaper picture. It portrayed a young man, slim, handsome, dark haired, but he had a pimple on the side of his nose, and a slight cast in his eye.

'Yes, that's him,' said Snowy. 'That's him, but he's grown a beard since then.'

'Are you sure? Are you positive?'

'Positive!' said Snowy. 'I can tell by the upper part of his face.'

Nobby put his grubby little paw over the picture of the man's chin. 'Hey, you're right, Snowy. It is old pimple-face himself.'

'Thank you very much,' said the policeman, folding up the newspaper. 'That's just what we want to know.' The policeman glanced at his patrol car driver. 'What do you think, Bert? Sounds like the Highwayman, doesn't it?'

'Could be, could be. What do you want to do, pull him in?'

'You bet your life I do. Come on, Bert. Cunning devil, under our noses all the time, disguised himself as a down-and-out, and all the time he's got two thousand pounds stacked away somewhere.'

'He had a bundle of five-pound notes,' said Snowy. 'We saw them on the bus.'

'That settles it,' said the policeman.

The policemen couldn't get out of the room fast enough. Mrs White went to show them out. Nobby almost choked. He glanced at the newspaper and found his voice.

'Highwayman, highwayman?' he said. 'That's no highwayman. He doesn't look a bit like Dick Turpentine to me. What's . . . what's he talking about?'

The newspaper referred to a criminal who had robbed a number of all-night garages of two thousand pounds.

'I don't know,' said Snowy. 'That's not our concern now. But I know one thing. You've messed up your film. You should not let the light get on an exposed film before it is developed to fix the picture images. How do you expect to get any prints off a blank film.'

'Oh, I don't know. If I brush my teeth every night without being told, and wash myself and go to bed really early, say five o'clock, maybe my dad will start my pocket money again.' Nobby looked at Snowy's watch. 'Wow, it's seven o'clock already. I'd better be off. I want to stay in Dad's good books for the next few years.'

Half-way through the night, Snowy was roused by his father.

'Listen, son,' said his father. 'I want you to do something for me. I want you to come down to the police station to identify a man they've just arrested. Will you do that?'

Snowy rubbed the sleep out of his eyes.

'He's a dangerous criminal, but you've nothing to be afraid of. I'll be with you all the time, and the police will be there too. The police car is waiting outside now.'

'Sure, Dad,' said Snowy.

Snowy was wide awake with excitement. He was bundled into his Cub's uniform and anorak, and driven in the waiting police car via the Clarks' house, where they picked up Nobby. At the police station they were brought before a line of men and asked to pick out the man who had chased them in the park.

'That's him,' said Snowy.

'No doubt about it,' said Nobby. 'His pimple sticks out farther than his nose.'

The police sergeant strolled over to the tramp. 'It's pretty obvious why you wanted to stop the boys taking your picture, isn't it, Briggs? With half the police in the county after you, you didn't want anyone to get a good look at your disguise.'

Suddenly the tramp broke out of the line and lunged at Nobby, but he was restrained by two policemen.

'Take him to the cells,' ordered the sergeant.

'I've never seen them before,' yelled the tramp as he was dragged away. 'It's only their word against mine. They're telling lies.'

'Cubs don't tell lies,' said Nobby, 'so there!'

'Of course they don't,' said the police sergeant, 'and neither does any decent man. You boys are a credit to the community. You've helped us a lot. The least I can do to repay you is to get the duty driver to run you home now.'

So the Cubs were driven home in the back of the police car.

'It's been an exciting day,' said Snowy.

'Yeah,' said Nobby. 'I've never been up as late as this before.'

'Pity your prints didn't come out.'

76

'Ah, don't worry about that, Snowy. I know how to take photographs now. All I have to do is save up my pocket money to buy a film, then I can take a set of photographs so good that Akela will want to hang them on his bedroom walls.'

6

The making of a masterpiece

It is fairly safe to say that anyone who is interested in photography would be interested in pictures generally, and so it was with Snowy and Nobby.

There was a picture, or rather a safety poster, on the wall at headquarters, which could only be described as horrible, yet Snowy and Nobby and several other Cubs in the Pack had copies of it pinned on their bedroom walls. Other copies were hung up in school-rooms and waiting-rooms, and pasted on bill-boards, not only in Cheshire, but all over the country. The reason they were there at all was entirely due to the Cubs' interest in art.

Art was just as much a part of Cub Scout work as tying knots; in fact there was a Cub Scout Artist's badge. Snowy and Nobby both tried their hands at sketching. Snowy had six sketches in his book, showing a tulip from his garden, the sundial at school, a bicycle, a vase at home, a line of people at a bus stop and the stone bridge across the stream just outside headquarters. After he had carefully sketched his subjects, he had lightly painted in the shadows with a trace of grey water-colour and had finished off each picture by inking it in with black drawing-ink.

When Snowy showed his book to the Cubs, they all wanted to have a go. Even Akela was impressed by Snowy's handwork, and he promptly organised an outing to a local beauty spot by the canal, where any Cub who was interested could try out his hand. He could not have chosen a better day, and the sun was shining as Akela led the Pack along the canal path.

'And how long did you say you'd been keeping a sketch-book, Rembrandt?' Akela asked Nobby.

Nobby put his sketch-book between his knees, and his pencil stub and king-size cheese rubber under his cap to free his hands. He counted his fingers.

'Eight weeks and two thumbs,' he said. 'I mean, eight weeks and two days, same as Snowy. We both started together.'

Nobby picked up his sketch-book, which had dropped on the ground.

'How many sketches do you have?'

'None, really,' said Nobby reluctantly. 'Well, I must have done dozens, but none of them were any good, so I tore them up. I'm afraid it will take me another week or two before I can produce my first masterpiece.'

Nobby opened up his sketch-book to show Akela. So many pages had been torn out of the front of the book that none of the back pages were fastened. The wind caught the remaining three pages and scattered them back along the canal bank. The Cubs charged after them, leaving Akela marching along all by himself.

'Free paper,' yelled the Cubs. 'See who can get the biggest piece.'

Snowy retrieved one sheet of paper from the top of a hawthorn bush, another sheet blew into the canal, and the third piece was torn into shreds by four Cubs who tried to pick it up together. Snowy handed Nobby the surviving page.

'There you are, Nobby,' said Snowy. 'It's a bit messed up, but you can use my sketch-book if you're stuck.'

'Thanks, Snowy.'

Nobby stuffed the page up his jersey to keep it out of the wind and hurried to catch up Akela. When he caught up his Cub Scout Leader, he fished a piece of crumpled paper from his back pocket and opened it up carefully.

'Well, I did keep my best drawing,' said Nobby. 'I tried to draw an eagle sitting on a chimney, but I couldn't draw the chimney properly, and the paper tore where I tried to rub it out. I think it looks good though. It looks like a moth having a feed on the paper, doesn't it? All I have to do is to put a few more holes in it, and I think it will look quite realistic.'

'Is that what it is?' said Akela, striding ahead. 'You can sketch your second masterpiece when we get to the lock gates.'

Nobby carefully folded up his sketch and returned it to his back pocket.

80

'I've lost my pencil,' he groaned, searching through his pockets.

'It's under your cap,' said Snowy.

'Oh, so it is. Thanks, Snowy.' Nobby looked at his little pencil stub, no bigger than his thumb. 'You wouldn't believe this was a new pencil before I sharpened it this morning, would you?'

The Cubs hurried to catch Akela, who had just stepped on to the footbridge on top of the lock gates.

'Don't fall in, lads,' warned Akela. 'This canal is dangerous, and the timber is rotten. Remember it is better to go home safely and have fish for your supper than feed yourselves to the fishes.'

'I thought fishes only ate worms,' said Nobby.

'Then they'd find you very tasty,' said Akela, over his shoulder. 'Hey, lads, look,' he went on. 'There's a real artist.'

The Cubs looked over the bridge parapet to the canal bank. True enough, on the grass verge overhanging the canal, they saw the artist standing before his easel and canvas, with his brushes and paint palette in his hands. Akela waved to the artist as he crossed over the bridge. The man was a retired headmaster from the local school.

Nobby grinned at the artist. 'Look your best,' he grunted to Snowy between clenched teeth. 'We are being painted for posterity.'

'He doesn't want to paint you,' said Snowy.

But Nobby ignored Snowy. He took off his cap

and combed his thick ginger hair with his fingers.

'Is my hair tidy?' he shouted at the artist. 'Is it all right, eh? Am I standing in the best position for you?'

The artist snorted and glowered at them through his thick glasses. Snowy could sense his frustration as he was disturbed by the Pack of noisy Cubs, but the artist retaliated by playing Nobby at his own game. He held out his brush at Nobby, as if measuring his proportions, then he stood up to make sure the Cubs could see him. He moved first to one side, then to the other as he pretended to find the best angle for his subject. But he was standing too close to the edge of the bank for such manoeuvres. Suddenly he overbalanced. He grabbed at his easel for support, but he tipped it over. His arms flayed like windmill sails, then, with a yell, he toppled into the water.

'Man overboard!' whooped Nobby. 'Depth charges a-way!'

'Throw him a lifebelt,' shouted Snowy. 'Quickly! I'll get Akela.'

Leaving Nobby to provide assistance, Snowy dashed across the lock bridge to find his Cub Scout Leader.

'Akela! Akela!' he shouted. 'There's a man in the canal. He needs help.'

Akela had settled down his Pack of Cubs, and was showing those gathered round him how to sketch. As soon as he heard Snowy's cries, he threw down the sketch-book, jumped up and dashed to the lock gates. Snowy doubled back after him, with the Cubs following behind like a pack of yelping hounds.

The artist had lost his spectacles, and was spluttering and floundering helplessly in the slimy waters. Nobby had already unstowed the lifebelt. He heaved it over the bridge parapet to the swimmer in distress. The lifebelt coiled through the air and hit the artist on the head.

'What are you trying to do, kill him?' barked Akela angrily.

'I . . . I was only trying to lasso him,' said Nobby faintly.

But Akela wasn't listening. He leapt on to the parapet, and after a quick glance to size up the situation, he dived into the canal. He reached the artist, then, giving a perfect exhibition of life-saving techniques, he rolled the man on to his back and tugged him gently towards the canal bank. The Cubs cheered and ran to the bank to help them out of the water.

The man spluttered and coughed, but managed to pull himself up on to dry land with the help of the Cubs.

'Are you all right?' asked Akela, coming up beside him.

'My clothes are ruined,' the man groaned, as the dirty, sticky water dripped off him. He peeled off his wet jacket and sweater and untied his collar.

'Can I do anything for you, mister?' asked Snowy. 'Can I ring for a taxi to take you home?'

'No, no, boy. That's my cottage just over there.' The man looked at Akela. 'You're in the same mess as I am, young man. Come with me to the cottage to change out of your wet things.'

Akela screwed up his shirt to squeeze out the water. 'Thank you for your offer, but I'd rather stay with my Cubs. It's pretty dangerous here, and if I turned my back for five minutes, one of them might fall in – Clark, for instance. But if you don't mind, I'd like to borrow a dry towel.'

'Please yourself. I know what you mean. If you let me take one of your Cubs, I'll send him back with a couple of towels.' The man rubbed his head. 'Something must have biffed me on the head. Can't think what, but I've got a lump the size of a boiled egg.'

Nobby slunk inside his neckerchief and turned to help the Cubs who were fishing the lifebelt and easel out of the water. The canvas, on its frame, had floated across to the lock gates, but Snowy retrieved it by climbing down the stout timbers and scooping it out of the water. The painting was ruined. Snowy took the soggy canvas back to the artist.

'Drowning in this canal must be a very unpleasant death,' said Akela.

'Yes, yes,' said the artist firmly. 'I can swim reasonably well, but I'm afraid I panicked in the water. Had you not pulled me out, I might have drowned. I can see now why young children drown so easily.'

Snowy held out the dripping canvas to the artist. 'Your painting is ruined,' he said.

'Well, I'm not much of an artist,' said the man modestly. 'I was only doing this to get some ideas for a safety advert. . . .' Suddenly he stopped talking. He goggled at the canvas held before him. 'Why . . . why that's just what it looks like from the water, with all that green slimy stuff over your head, and a dim view of the lock behind. Why, this is a masterpiece.'

'Masterpiece?' sniffed Nobby. 'I didn't know you had to dip paintings in water to make masterpieces.'

The man was really excited by now. 'Look,' he said, showing them all his canvas. 'Look at this picture. Can't you feel that you are up to your eyeballs in the canal? Can't you feel you are on the verge of drowning?'

'Ugh! It makes me feel sick,' said Nobby.

'That's just it!' said the man. 'That's it, that's it! It makes you want to retch up the dirty water in your throat.' The man picked up his easel and folding stool and tucked them under his arms. He nodded to Akela. 'Thank you for saving my life, for what it's worth. What is more important, you've probably helped to save the lives of children who would otherwise drown in canals all over the country. I'll send you some dry clothes and a towel.' The man chuckled and squelched off towards his cottage. 'This is a winner,' he said to himself, 'just what I wanted.'

'Funny bird,' muttered Akela, turning away.

'If I didn't know him, I'd swear that lump on his head had made him simple. Okay, fellows, back to your sketch-books. The swimming gala is over now.'

The Cubs went back to their places. Snowy made a sketch of Nobby dipping his moth-eaten drawing in the water. After dipping his drawing and rubbing it in the dirt, Nobby angrily screwed it up and flung it out into the canal in disgust. He came and plonked himself down beside Snowy.

'My drawing was a masterpiece before I dipped it in the canal, now . . . now it's ruined.' He sighed and looked over Snowy's shoulder. 'Hey, Snowy, what's that you are drawing, a ballet-dancer? There are no ballet-dancers around here, are there?'

'They are the rough guide lines of what is supposed to be a sketch of you,' said Snowy.

Snowy filled in a little more detail and a picture gradually emerged of a Cub bending over the canal.

'Cor, you're a good artist,' said Nobby. 'I wish I could draw like that.'

'I've got a book out of the library on how to draw. It's got all the instructions in. Do you want to borrow it?'

'Oh, thanks, Snowy.'

Snowy wrote the date in the corner of his sketch and closed his book. When he got home, he would have another look at it. It would, of course, be better when it was finished in ink and wash.

'Pack it up now, lads,' said Akela, putting out the fire. 'You've had half an hour. Time to back-track to headquarters. Hurry up now. I need a hot shower.'

'I'll say you do,' said Nobby, nipping his nose. 'You are beginning to smell a bit.'

The Cubs thought they had heard the last of the artist, but a month later they received a letter from him with a copy of his new advertisement poster. Properly printed, the poster was most impressive. It made a strong impact as a warning to children of the dangers of playing near unfenced canals. Apparently fifty thousand copies had already been circulated to schools and youth organisations all over the country. It even impressed the Advertising Council, who voted it one of the ten best advertising campaigns of the year.

There was little doubt that the campaign would save lives, and that is the main reason why the poster on the wall at headquarters is a prized possession. Besides that, it was also a reminder to the Cubs of their afternoon by the canal, when they helped to make a masterpiece.

7

Snowy plays his part

Photography, art, handcraft, making collections, and all the many other activities of Cub work were interesting in themselves, but what made Cub life so fascinating to Snowy and Nobby were the unusual, sometimes quite unexpected adventures in which they were involved. There were many adventures, but the one Snowy and Nobby will never forget, even if they each reach the age of ninety, is that which started out as a normal local interest expedition. It was a cold, windy day, not that that was likely to put off any of the 2nd Billington Cub Scout Pack.

'Line up, lads. Be smart about it,' said Akela to his Pack. The Cubs lined up in a manor house courtyard. 'For those interested, as part of your Silver Arrow test, you are to visit a local place of historical interest and tell the Pack about it. Now this hall is very interesting. Queen Elizabeth I slept here in 1592, and Sir Francis Drake in 1587. Inside the hall you will see many genuine Elizabethan objects and works of art, so take note of anything which interests you, then next Cub night you can tell your story if you want to take your test. There is another point I want to make. There are other visitors to this hall, and a film unit is working in the west wing; so keep out of their way, and don't make nuisances of yourselves. I want you to be on your best behaviour. Remember you are all members of the 2nd Billington Cub Scout Pack, and I want you to keep up its good name. Understand? Any questions?'

'Is it haunted?' asked Nobby. 'The house, I mean?'

Akela laughed. 'As a matter of fact it is supposed to be. In 1531, the local squire, Sir Charles Prior, was beheaded in this forecourt just about where you are standing now, Nobby. His ghost is reputed to haunt this place on the thirteenth day of the month.'

'That's today,' said Snowy.

'Why did you say that?' said Nobby, shaking like a jelly. 'Do you want to give me hysterics? I can already feel my hair standing on end. If I see a ghost, I'll jump out of my skin.'

'If a ghost sees you, he'll jump out of his skeleton, or whatever ghosts can jump out of. Now file inside quietly, the lot of you,' said Akela. 'Don't touch any of the exhibits, or I'll have you locked up in the dungeon.'

'I wish I had gone to the cinema instead,' said Nobby, clinging on to Snowy as the Cubs filed into the manor hall. 'There's a good film showing at the Astra, *The Monster from 5000*

Fathoms. It will be better than this creepy place.'

The guide led the Pack through the gloomy stateroom, up the creaking stairs and into a low-beamed bedroom. On one wall was a dark mirror set in an elaborately carved frame which formed part of an oak dressing-table and seat assembly. Nobby looked into the dark mirror and grinned.

'Hello, Handsome,' he said to his reflection. He combed his thick ginger hair with his fingers. 'Your hair is a bit scruffy, your nose is too small, your teeth are too big and your ears stick out, but I love you just the same.'

'That mirror has seen one of the most horrifying cut-throats of all time,' said the guide.

'What do you mean?' said Nobby hotly. 'I'm not *that* ugly.'

The guide turned and pointed to the four-poster bed. 'On the night of 13 November 1526, a young boy was sleeping in this bed. Into this bedroom, on the stroke of midnight, crept an intruder. No one knows how he came, because the hall and the stateroom below were crowded with guests, and no one saw him enter or leave. So this man, undetected in the dark, crept up to the bed, put his hands around the little boy's throat and strangled him. . . .'

'W . . . w . . . w . . . w . . . whow!' moaned Nobby.

'Several other murders occurred in the following months,' went on the guide, 'and they

all happened on the night of the thirteenth of the
month. And although the manor was crowded
with guests, banqueting and feasting on each
occasion, no one ever saw the intruder. At one
time, Sir Charles Prior posted guards outside the
door, but still the murders went on. . . .'

'I think I'm going to faint,' said Nobby weakly.
His legs buckled under him, and he collapsed on
the dressing-table seat before the dark mirror. He
nudged Snowy. 'Tell him to shut up. He's giving
me an attack of the collywobbles.'

'The intruder was finally caught in this room
on his thirteenth attempt, and he turned out to
be Sir Charles Prior himself,' said the guide. 'He
wouldn't say how he had entered the room, and
that remains a mystery to this day. Next let me
show you the picture gallery.'

Nobby slouched on the dressing-table seat,
too weak to move, as the guide led the Cubs'

party out of the bedroom. Snowy stayed behind with him.

'He shouldn't be allowed to frighten people like that,' said Nobby, trying to regain control of himself.

Snowy wasn't listening. 'Look at these carvings,' said Snowy excitedly. 'They must have taken ages to make. Isn't this mirror a marvellous topic for the local interest story? Just imagine, Nobby. This mirror has been here for over four hundred years. Just imagine all that it has seen. It must have seen the murders!'

Nobby flopped across the dressing-table. 'Don't you start,' he moaned. 'Let . . . l . . . let's get out of here.'

He gripped a carved candlestick holder on the frame of the mirror to pull himself to his feet. The thing twisted in his hand, and the whole mirror, dressing-table and seat assembly swung round, taking the boys with it.

'Yeowh!' yelled Nobby.

Before they realised what was happening, Snowy and Nobby were carried around into a jet-black darkness behind the wall panel. The panel clicked shut, and they were locked inside.

'Where . . . where . . . are we?' whimpered Nobby. 'Let me out, let me out. I want my mum.'

In an instant, Snowy was on his feet, feeling the cold, smooth mirror which now sealed them off from the bedroom.

'We . . . we can't get out!' he gasped. 'We . . . we're locked in.'

'I want to be locked out,' yelled Nobby. 'I told you we should have gone to the cinema. Help! Help!'

The chamber was black and dirty.

'No one can hear us in here,' said Snowy. 'There's no one in the bedroom now, either. No one will hear us.'

'What . . . what do we do?' asked Nobby. 'Mum said I hadn't to be late for tea.'

'We must be in a secret passage. We'll have to find another way out. Come on, Nobby. Let's get out of here as quickly as we can. There must be another way out.'

Snowy led the way, groping along the dirty, grimy, cobwebby wall. A spider crawled over his arm. He shook it to the ground. It suddenly occurred to him that this passageway must have been used by Sir Charles Prior to go undetected into the bedroom.

'The strangler must have used this route,' said Snowy.

He felt a firm hand grip him by the shoulder and hot breath on the back of his neck.

'Don't . . . don't . . . say that,' said Nobby in his ear. 'Say you're only joking, Snowy. Tell me you're kidding.'

'Let go of me, Nobby. You nearly frightened me to death.'

Snowy groped on, in complete darkness, until eventually he saw a tiny shaft of light, like a long pencil, coming through a hole in the wall. Snowy groped on until he reached the light, then he bent down and peered through the crack. He could see straight down into another room. He was amazed by what he saw.

Snowy could see straight into a drawing-room. There, a lady dressed in rich Elizabethan gowns stood by a dark polished table. Before her stood a ruffian, with a drawn sword. Slowly the ruffian raised the blade of his sword, and put the point on the lady's neck. Snowy rubbed his eyes, for he could not believe what he could see. He wondered if he was now part of another, ghostly, world.

'What can you see, Snowy?'

'I'm going bonkers,' said Snowy.

'I've been trying to tell you that for ages.'

Snowy looked again. By now the lady had been pushed back against the oak-panelled wall, but she could retreat no further.

'You must leave this house at once,' she said.

'Leave? Not before I've seen the end of you, Lady Anne, you witch. Was it not by your orders that I was flung, in chains, into the dungeon? It's your turn now to plead for mercy.'

The lady knocked aside the sword blade. 'Go away!' she screamed. 'Leave me alone. Help! Help! Father!'

Nobby pushed Snowy away from the crack.

'Let me see.' Nobby peeped through the crack. 'Wow!' he gasped. 'I'm going bonkers now. We've . . . we've been transported back into history. It . . . it doesn't make sense.'

It did not make sense to Snowy either. He rubbed his fingers over the panelled wall and discovered that some of it was stretched canvas. He groped around further, hoping to find a way out. All this time, the lady and the villain continued to shout at each other. Suddenly the lady screamed.

'He's stabbed her, he's stabbed her,' shrieked Nobby. 'The rotten dog.'

Snowy and Nobby tried to look through the small crack together. There was not much room for such manoeuvres and suddenly the panel splintered and collapsed, and their secret passageway was flooded with light. Snowy fell to his knees to stop himself falling through the torn canvas opening. Nobby went straight through the opening, head first.

'Wow!' yelled Nobby, in despair.

When Snowy opened his eyes, he saw that Nobby had fallen across the boom microphone of a modern sound-recorder unit. Nobby, meanwhile, clung to the microphone for dear life. A sound technician tried to swing the boom out of harm's way, which was the last thing in the world he should have done. Nobby was as black as soot, for the secret passageway had been as grimy as a chimney. He hung on to the boom like a monkey hanging from a branch. As he swung across the room, he collided with film cameras and spotlights, sending them crashing around the technicians, who, when they tried to get out of his way, tripped over the cables and sent more equipment crashing on to the floor. Only after he had thumped into the wall did Nobby drop off the boom.

They had, in fact, broken into the drawing-room in the west wing of the manor hall. The near half of the drawing-room was filled with film cameras, sound recording equipment, spotlights and technicians. At the far side of the room, Lady Anne lay on the floor, the top of her dress stained with what looked like blood. The ruffian turned at the interruption.

'What's going on here?' yelled the director angrily.

The leading actress picked herself up and stalked across the equipment-strewn floor to where Nobby sat with his back against the wall.

'You horrible, filthy little boy,' she snapped. 'How dare you ruin my scene?'

Nobby grinned up at her. 'You . . . you're still alive!' he said in amazement.

'Does that disappoint you?' she shrieked. 'Did you come here to murder the lot of us?'

'It's . . . it's all a mistake,' said Snowy from the hole in what used to be a portrait of Queen Elizabeth I.

'Mistake?' shrieked the actress. 'Ooooh!'

The film director pushed aside a fallen spotlight and got up from the floor. He flung away his squashed cigar.

'What are you doing up there, you menace?' he yelled at Snowy, still framed in the oil painting.

Snowy climbed through the picture frame. Nobby clambered over the wrecked film equipment.

'We didn't mean to interrupt,' said Snowy, wiping his hands on his handkerchief. 'It was an accident. We were lost in a secret passageway.'

'Well get lost some other place,' yelled the actress. 'Do you realise that you've almost wrecked this crummy picture?'

'What do you mean, "crummy picture"?' snapped the director, turning on her sharply.

'Mean? What I say. This is a crummy picture. A crummy plot, crummy dialogue, crummy everything – including, I might add, a crummy director.'

'And a crummy actress,' added the director viciously.

'Oh!' The actress almost choked. 'Oh! Well, if that's how you feel, I'm leaving. This is the last straw. I can find work elsewhere. I don't rely on you for a part. Don't ask me to come back, for I won't, ever. I was talked into doing this picture against my better judgement. You can keep your crummy film. I'm going back to television.'

With that, the actress picked up her skirts and flounced out of the room. Her leading man ran after her, to try to make her change her mind.

'Think of the money you're throwing away,' he screeched. 'We're all in this together.'

'Money? I could earn more money washing dishes. If you stay with this crummy company, you'll go bankrupt with them.'

In the midst of all this devastation, the director fumed.

'Prima donnas,' he yelled after them. 'Fairies, nincompoops.'

'We were lost in a secret passage,' said Nobby. 'We didn't mean to wreck your crummy picture.'

The film director almost exploded. 'Crummy picture? Don't you start.' He glowered at his technicians. 'Does anyone else think my picture is crummy? How does anyone know if my picture is crummy before they see it?' The technicians did not reply. Some of them shuffled uneasily. The director lowered his eyes. The truth, it seemed, was dawning on him. 'Well, perhaps it is. I should never have started a sloppy historical romance in the first place.'

The film director looked a lonely and disappointed man. He walked over the empty stage.

'Lots of people like historical romances,' said Snowy, brushing himself down. 'I like historical pictures myself.'

'Especially if there's lots of fencing in them,' said Nobby, 'and ghosts.'

Suddenly the director burst into laughter. 'You're a couple of clowns,' he said. Then he snapped his fingers. 'But you've given me an idea. Say, can you boys act?'

'I don't know,' said Nobby. 'I've never tried.'

'Maybe you can learn now. We can coach you in stage-craft. All you have to do to be a great actor is to be natural. How would you boys like a part in a new film? I've had an idea in the back of

100

my mind for years. It's a comedy . . . about a haunted house. People love comedies. Would you boys like to give it a try?'

'If you think so,' said Snowy.

The film director turned to his producer. 'Wrap it up, Louis. Get the scriptwriters to work on a new comedy script. Tell them to make room for two nine-year-old clowns in the cast.' The director picked up a couple of scripts from the floor. 'Here, boys, let me give you a film test.' He gave a copy of the script to Nobby. 'You play Jasper,' he said. 'That's your part. Read from the top of the page. And you, Blondie,' he said to Snowy, 'you take the lead. Right? Read on, Ginger Nut.'

Nobby looked at his script. 'I am going to take you with me,' read Nobby. 'I'll take you away where no one will ever find us.'

Snowy looked at his lines next to the part labelled *Lady Anne*. He raised his sparkling blue eyes.

'I cannot come with you,' he said in a clear voice. 'My heart belongs to another. I can never, never marry you, never.'

Nobby dropped his script. 'What . . . what . . . do you mean, Snowy? You *have* gone bonkers! I don't want to marry you.'

'I'm only reading the script,' said Snowy. 'Don't you know anything about acting?'

The film director clapped his hands. 'Naturals, naturals,' he said in delight. 'You two are a couple of born actors. I can see this film in my mind. It will be great. You'll enjoy it.' He looked round. 'Hey, Louis, tell the scriptwriters to see me in my office. I want to fill them in on this new comedy idea of mine.'

So Snowy and Nobby were provisionally booked for the cast of the new film. That was six months ago. Since then they haven't heard from the film company. Perhaps it was decided that it wasn't a good idea after all. On the other hand, the scriptwriters could still be working on the story, in which case Snowy and Nobby might hear from the studios any day.

Snowy used his visit to the manor hall to pass the exploring part of his Silver Arrow, with an account of the discovery of the secret passage. He also gave an exhibition of acting in preparation for his film work. Nobby wasn't ready for any of the Silver Arrow tests. He did, however, offer to give demonstrations of mime and acting, but he messed up the first because he talked too much when he mimed, and the second because he lost his voice. So no one really knows what would happen if indeed he did get a film part.

8

Party piece

Snowy took his Cub tests in his stride. In less than a year, he had his Silver Arrow badge. Nobby, on the other hand, had the utmost difficulty in passing even the most basic tests. He knew the meaning of the Cub Scout Law and Promise well enough, and on one occasion had even recited them correctly to Akela. How he managed that, Akela was at a loss to understand, but he had to admit that Nobby was keen. And Nobby was always the first to congratulate any Cub awarded a badge, and never complained about being left behind. Yet, on more than one occasion, Snowy caught him looking at

his Silver Arrow with envious eyes, and Snowy, to his credit, never once bragged about it.

December came and the last Cub parade of the year was the night of the Cub Christmas party. All the Cubs were expecting a good time and Nobby dashed out of the house as soon as he saw Snowy coming to collect him. He slapped his pal's back.

'Hi, Snowman,' he grinned. 'All set for the party?'

'Sure.' Snowy noticed that Nobby had a couple of boxes under his arm. 'What have you got there, Nobby?'

Nobby showed him the boxes. 'This is a box of cakes, sandwiches and sausage rolls Mum got me for the party, and this is a box of cream biscuits I bought with my own pocket money. Well, it was a box of cream biscuits, but I tried a few of them to make sure they were all right. Would you like one, Snowy?'

'You'd better keep them for the party. Here, have one of my chocolate fingers. Go on, I have plenty, besides all this other stuff. It should be a great party, shouldn't it, Nobby?'

'You bet!'

The Cubs gathered at their headquarters, where they put up the trestle tables and set them with all the food they pooled together. Then they tucked in as though they hadn't eaten for a week. An hour later, the tables were clear. There was not a crumb left.

After the meal, Akela had arranged to show

his Cubs the film he had taken of their summer weekend camp. He switched out the lights and the film projector whirled. On the screen, as large as life, flashed Snowy, batting in the Cub cricket match. When the ball was played, he cut it off his leg side through the gully and shot off his mark to run. Next, Nobby came waddling into the picture in cricket pads two sizes too large for him, having left the smaller pair for Snowy.

Immediately every Cub watching the performance roared with laughter.

'There's the Monster from Five Thousand Fathoms,' yelled someone in the darkened hall.

In the film, Nobby took up his stance, looking more like a gawky camel than a batsman. The ball dropped short, but Nobby stepped back and knocked out his leg stump. Then he swung his bat back ready to knock the ball for six. Instead, the bat slipped out of his hand and shot over the wicket-keeper's head. The ball then hit Nobby on the back of the neck; he tripped over his two remaining stumps and sat on the wicket-keeper. The film was unfair, however, for in that innings, Nobby had scored fifteen runs, second only to Snowy's score of twenty-one.

The Cubs thought the film was extremely funny, and strange to say, so did Nobby himself, in the front row. Perhaps that was not so strange after all, for Nobby had always been the first to laugh at himself. He wasn't the least bit sad – in fact he laughed more than any of the Pack. And

when Akela showed the film through a second time, Nobby laughed twice as much. It was, he confessed, the best film he had ever seen, better even than *The Monster from 5000 Fathoms*.

The film ended with Nobby hoisting his trousers up the flagpole to dry as the other Cubs stood to attention and saluted. His trousers had got soaked when he had jumped accidentally into a horse trough whilst demonstrating he could clear it with his eyes closed. The film did not, however, show him in the horse trough.

After the film show, the lights were switched on and Akela called his Cubs to attention. He held up a bright and shiny silver cup.

'This is the Cheshire Cub Scout Cup,' he said, holding up the trophy proudly, 'which has been awarded this year to the 2nd Billington Cub Scout Pack.'

The Cubs cheered and stamped their feet.

'This cup was awarded to us, and, I might add, against the competition of over a hundred other Cub Scout Packs, in recognition of our achievements in sport, activities and proficiency tests over the past year. This cup was won by the individual efforts and teamwork of all of you. This cup belongs to every member of the Pack, but I can't chop it up into thirty-six pieces and give you a piece each. It is also too valuable to leave here at headquarters. The usual arrangement, in this case, is for the cup to be given to a trustworthy Cub for safe keeping, but to save any argument, I'll pick the names of twelve Cubs from a hat. Each Cub will be allowed to keep the cup for one month, in the order as drawn out of the hat. Right? Now each one of you has been given a piece of paper by his Sixer. On that paper, write your name, fold up the paper and put it in my beret on the table.'

Each Cub wrote down his name, and the Sixers collected the papers and put them in Akela's beret.

'Any more?' said Akela, giving his beret a good shake.

There were no more names to be added. Akela drew a paper from the hat. The Cubs were silent as he opened the paper.

'For January,' he called out. 'Nobby Clark!'

'Good old Nobby,' shouted the Cubs, applauding wildly.

Akela looked at the name closely. 'You surprise me, Nobby, how neatly you write! Anyway, you'll keep the cup for January.' Akela gave the names another little shake and withdrew another name. 'For February,' he said: 'N. Clark. Hey, what's going on?'

'I suppose someone thought Nobby, as the best Cub in the Pack, deserves to keep the cup....' explained Snowy.

'Nobby, the best Cub in the Pack?' echoed Akela. 'Clown Prince of Cubs, you mean.' Akela took another name from the hat. 'For March – Nobby.' Akela goggled at the name. 'What's this, a conspiracy?' He looked at another name, and another, and another. 'April – Nob, May – Nobby Clark, June – Nobby C., July – Nobby, August, September, October, November . . . All Nobby! Hey, these are all Nobby Clark!'

The Cubs stamped and cheered wildly. The noise was so great that the floor shook and the windows rattled. The applause went on for fully five minutes, and eventually Akela had to blow his whistle four times to quieten them. Nobby could hardly believe his ears. He looked about him.

'Is there another Nobby in the Pack?' he asked.

Akela held up his hands. 'All right, Cubs, I get your point. What you are saying in effect is that you think Nobby Clark is the best Cub in the Pack, and he deserves to keep the cup for a whole year, right? Well, that's very sporting of you, but let me give you my views. I don't believe any Cub is any better or any worse than the next Cub, but I've got to admit that there could only be one Nobby Clark. There could only be one in the world like you.' Akela ruffled Nobby's ginger hair and looked over his head. 'I entirely agree with your verdict, lads, and I'm sure B-P himself would approve of your sporting gesture. Nobby Clark is one of the nicest little fellows it has ever been my honour to meet. In times of difficulty, we can always rely on that foghorn laugh of his to get us out of trouble.'

The Cubs cheered again as Akela presented the cup to Nobby. Snowy put his arm around his pal's shoulders.

'Quiet, quiet!' shouted Akela at the top of his

voice. He blew a long blast on his whistle. At last the noise subsided. Akela waited until he could hear a pin drop. 'Now we will ask Nobby to do us the honour of lowering the flag on the last Cub night of the year,' he said calmly and seriously.

The Cubs formed their circles and stood to attention as Nobby proudly lowered the flag. After they broke away, the Cubs cheered again.

'Chair him now, Cubs,' shouted Snowy.

The Cubs rushed at Nobby, hoisted him on their shoulders and carried him in triumph out of the building. Nobby was overwhelmed. They carried him over the stone bridge and set him down safely by the telephone box.

'Thanks, lads,' said Nobby. 'For a moment I thought you were going to throw me in the stream. I've . . . I've really enjoyed being with you in the Cubs. I really mean that.'

Snowy gave Nobby a friendly nudge in the ribs. 'You've won the cup this year, Nobby. What do you plan to win next year?'

'The saucer to go with it,' said Nobby.

More Beaver Books

We hope you have enjoyed this Beaver Book. Here are some of the other titles.

Crazy Misstakes A Beaver original. A hilarious collection of howlers and clangers from newspapers, the classroom, advertisements, translations and public notices, collected by Janet Rogers and guaranteed to amuse you for hours; illustrated by David Mostyn

Explore a Castle An exciting and original book which helps readers to work out how castles functioned and how people lived in them, including a special section on making a superb model castle of your own. Written by Brian Davison and illustrated with photographs and line drawings

Henry and the Clubhouse All Henry Huggins really wants to do is make a success of his paper round and help his friends build a clubhouse, but with Ramona around even the best intentions go awry! A very funny book for readers of eight upwards by Beverly Cleary with illustrations by Thelma Lambert

These and many other Beavers are available from your local bookshop or newsagent, or can be ordered direct from: Hamlyn Paperback Cash Sales, PO Box 11, Falmouth, Cornwall TR10 9EN. Send a cheque or postal order for the price of the book plus postage at the following rates:
UK: 45p for the first book, 20p for the second book, and 14p for each additional book ordered to a maximum charge of £1.63;
BFPO and Eire: 45p for the first book, 20p for the second book, plus 14p per copy for the next 7 books and thereafter 8p per book;
OVERSEAS: 75p for the first book and 21p for each extra book.

New Beavers are published every month and if you would like the *Beaver Bulletin*, a newsletter which tells you about new books and gives a complete list of titles and prices, send a large stamped addressed envelope to:

Beaver Bulletin
Arrow Books Limited
17–21 Conway Street
London W1P 5HL

9332205